GOD
CAN DO IT
AGAIN

GOD
CAN DO IT
AGAIN

Amazing testimonies wrought by God's extraordinary servant

Kathryn Kuhlman

Bridge-Logos *Publishers*

Gainesville, Florida 32614 USA

Cover photograph by Doug Grandstaff

God Can Do It Again
by Kathryn Kuhlman
Copyright © 1969 by The Kathryn Kuhlman Foundation
Revised edition 1993
Reprinted 2002
Library of Congress Catalog Card Number: 93-71949
International Standard Book Number: 0-88270-710-8

Published by:
Bridge-Logos *Publishers*
P.O. Box 141630
Gainesville, FL 32614
http://www.bridgelogos.com

Contents

Introduction

In this moving and inspiring book, Miss Kuhlman has brought together the first-person stories of several who have been cured of ills ranging from multiple sclerosis to spiritual emptiness.

Each page radiates Miss Kuhlman's love of God and His love of all mankind.

These testimonies attest to God's wonder-working power and are a strong affirmation of Miss Kuhlman's conviction that *GOD CAN DO IT AGAIN!*

Foreword

by Kathryn Kuhlman

If you never meet Kathryn Kuhlman, you will not have missed a thing. If you are seeking a faith healer, read no further. If you are in search of a profound theology, this book is definitely not a textbook. Is it a new religion or sensation you want? Then I surely cannot help you. I have no new religion to offer. I am not a modern day seer nor am I a worker of miracles.

Kathryn Kuhlman is just a woman. No one knows better than I that in myself, I am nothing. I am not your point of contact. I am not a deliverer. I stand before you helpless and yet the miracles happen. Why—why?

I marvel just as you will marvel, I weep just as you will weep; I rejoice just as you will rejoice as through the pages of this book you begin to catch a glimpse of the awesome love and power of God Almighty as He touches and moves in His sovereignty.

The people come. And in their desperation they seek answers.

"Why am I so ill?" people ask.

"If God loves me, why did He take my child?"

"I have cancer and I am afraid to die. What can I do?"

"My husband is mentally depressed. Our home, our marriage, is just miserable."

"I have prayed for my healing and I believe that God can heal. Why am I not healed?"

How would you answer them? How can I answer them? I would give my life—my life—if that would be the answer.

In the great miracle services in Los Angeles, in Pittsburgh, no matter in which city, there are thousands of people who come expecting me to work that miracle they seek. But I have nothing whatsoever to do with what happens. I am just as amazed and thrilled as anyone else when the service begins and God works His wonders in the midst of us all.

The Holy Spirit, the Third Person of the Trinity, comes in power and He uses the vessel yielded unto Him. I cannot use the Holy Spirit, He must use me. It is not so important that I touch anyone, but rather that the Holy Spirit touch the life, the heart, and fill the individual with himself.

A body made whole by the power of God is a great miracle of God's love and mercy. But the greatest miracle of all is a heart made clean by the blood of Jesus Christ—a soul born again by the Holy Spirit, born into the family of God, our Heavenly Father, made an heir and joint-heir with our precious Lord and Saviour, Jesus Christ. That God should love us so much—this is the miracle of all miracles.

You ask me for answers. I have only one: Jesus Christ. He is the answer, no matter what the question may be.

As for Kathryn Kuhlman, I am just a child of my Heavenly Father because of Jesus Christ, and without the Holy Spirit I am nothing—nothing. How can I help but say, "Thank you, Jesus—thanks a million!"

Kathryn Kuhlman

1

Miracles Do Happen—
A Reporter's Account
by Jamie Buckingham

It was ten o'clock Sunday morning in the city of Los Angeles—the day of the miracle service.

I was standing on the sidewalk outside the seven thousand seat Shrine Auditorium where Kathryn Kuhlman holds her monthly services. I could hardly believe my eyes. Although the service was not scheduled to begin until 2 P.M., the sidewalks and porches already were jammed with waiting people.

Young men with fuzzy hair and uncombed beards rubbed shoulders with dignified matrons who arrived in chauffeur-driven limousines. There were suburban housewives, businessmen, Hollywood personalities, young couples with children, doctors, nurses, and the ever-present sick. Many had flown in from Seattle, Portland, Las Vegas, Houston, Denver. Some, I learned, came every month from Hawaii and British Columbia.

Chartered buses from hundreds of miles around were arriving by the minute and after alighting the passengers stood in groups with signs to identify their location—Santa Barbara, San Diego, Sacramento. More than fifty buses arrived before the service started. I wandered from one end of the block to the other shaking my head in disbelief.

I was in Los Angeles to observe one of the miracle services which have become a regular part of the Kathryn Kuhlman ministry. In a time when most churches compete with golf courses and lakes for their members' presence on Sunday morning, and when many others have turned off their lights on Sunday night, Kathryn Kuhlman's meetings are always so crowded that there is standing room only.

I had discovered the secret just a month before, when I stood on the steps of the old Carnegie Hall in Pittsburgh to attend the Friday morning miracle service at Miss Kuhlman's home base. There, I had talked to many persons who let nothing keep them from attending the miracle services. They come, the physically healthy, to share in the joy of God's love and mercy. And, of course, those in physical desperation come in droves to wait and pray for their personal miracles.

The crowd in Pittsburgh was much like the crowd in Los Angeles. I saw chartered buses from Ohio and Kentucky, cars from Ontario; pickup trucks from West Virginia were parked beside Cadillacs from Delaware. I talked with a group of theology students from Harvard's Divinity School in Boston. They had come to observe and scoff, but went away believing.

The sick were there in great numbers. One woman, huddled beside the building on a folding chair, told me she had been there since dawn. She had ridden the bus from Indianapolis all night, coming to be healed of stomach cancer.

I made my way through the crowd of wheel hairs on the side porch and slipped through the back door of the auditorium. Behind the stage in a small passageway, Kathryn Kuhlman was pacing back and forth, her face uplifted in prayer and her lips moving without audible sound. She was completely oblivious to the others around her as she talked with God. When at last she saw me, we exchanged quick greetings. Shaking my head, I began to remark about the sights I had seen on the front steps. "I saw a child...."

She interrupted me with a compassionate, "Please...I have a service to do." Her soft blue eyes searched my face for a moment. "No one knows better than I how powerless I am," she said, her voice now filled with emotion, "how dependent I am on the mercy of the Lord to help these precious people. But the ability of God is beyond our comprehension, beyond our strongest faith, beyond our largest prayers.

"Come with me," she said suddenly. Grabbing my hand she led me briskly toward the little door that opened onto the stage. "There! See those three steps. See that black doorknob. I die a thousand deaths every time I go up those steps, turn that knob, and walk out onto that platform. There are thousands of people out there who have come in their desperation to be healed—to find God. But I cannot give them anything. Only the Holy Spirit can give it. I stand on these steps and you will never know how I feel when I open that door. I know people have come from great distances.

"I know this is their last hope. I have no power to heal. All that I can do is to remind them of the bigness of God, the greatness of God, that He is still God Almighty. I am only the vessel that is surrendered. God does the rest.

3

"Last week...no, it was two weeks ago, a man came back here before the service. We try to keep the people out of the wings before the service because they would overwhelm me. But he got back here and asked me to pray for his ear. He had cancer of the ear. I have never heard a man sob...cry...like that man. That is all he did. He did not pray. He just sobbed. We prayed a simple prayer and he left."

Her face was beaming as she continued excitedly: "Last week he was back and his ear was as pink and nice as can be. That is the power of God," she said as she broke into a prayer of thanksgiving. She turned and walked back down that long corridor, holding her hands up and praying for the anointing of God before the service began.

I squeezed through a door which carried me from the stage into the huge Shrine Auditorium in Los Angeles. It was already humming with activity. Some three hundred choir members were in their places rehearsing their numbers with energy and harmony.

Music plays a big part in the Kathryn Kuhlman services. Arthur Metcalfe, a distinguished musician with a doctor of philosophy degree from St. Olaf's, is the choir director. For many years he directed the Pittsburgh Civic Chorus and the Canterbury Choir before joining the Kuhlman organization. Wisely, he believes that music should reach the heart as well as the mind and offers a masterful blend of gospel music along with Mendelssohn and Bach.

Miss Kuhlman's long-time organist, Charles Beebee, was at the console. I knew that he would undergird the entire service with appropriate music. At one of the grand pianos sat Tom Murray, an intense young musician. I learned that he had quietly volunteered to sing in the choir several months earlier. That was before Dr. Metcalfe discovered that he was one of the most brilliant concert organists in California and the winner of several national awards. When approached about playing one of the pianos, he humbly consented, but refused to be recognized publicly.

Even before the doors were opened to the public, the atmosphere in the great auditorium was charged with excitement. The wheelchair sections in the side box seats were nearly filled. (Those in wheelchairs and on stretchers were allowed to come in early through a side door.) Everyone, from stage hands to choir members, seemed to recognize that before the afternoon was over this great auditorium would once again become the scene of miracles.

I took a seat on the platform along with several distinguished looking men. Suddenly the doors opened. The people poured in like water through the sluice gates of a great dam. They were actually running down the aisles to get close to the front. The ushers vainly tried to slow them down, but it was useless as the tide of humanity swept in, filling up the ground floor, swirling into the first balcony, mounting to the second and then the third.

Within ten minutes every seat in the vast auditorium was taken. It was hard to believe.

Dr. Metcalfe came back onto the stage. The choir exploded into song. "Exploded" is the only word for it as they rang out the sounds of "Pentecostal Fire." They did not just sing, they overflowed; they erupted in joyous acclamation of sound and harmony. The music pealed until the walls fairly vibrated and my scalp tingled.

After several anthems and choruses the choir began a song that has become a trademark among all those who

know of Miss Kuhlman's ministry: "He touched me...."
A stocky, middle-aged man with an intense face leaned
forward in his wheelchair near the stage and whispered
to his wife beside him, "That is her song...Miss Kuhlman's. Here she comes!"

Suddenly, a slim figure in a green silk dress appeared
on the platform. Her long auburn hair glistened under
the bright, colored lights. Her smile was captivating, en-
trancing. Electricity seemed to crackle from her. The congregation burst into thunderous applause, a spontaneous
demonstration of their love for her.

The ovation ceased abruptly as she led the crowd of
standing people in her theme song:

He touched me—Oh, He touched me.
And oh, the joy that floods my soul.
Something happened and now I know
He touched me—and made me whole.

We sang it once, twice, and over and over. Those
who were unfamiliar with the words or music were soon
swept up in the singing. Forgetting that I was there as
an objective reporter, I found myself singing with them.
A powerful ground swell of praise was rising.

Then Miss Kuhlman stopped singing and just stood
there before that great throng, her arms outstretched, her
face upturned, her eyes shut, her lips moving in prayer
as we sang on. Her face seemed to give off rays of light.
She appeared lost in her communion with God.

She moved forward and in her rich contralto voice
started singing a new refrain, "Then sings my soul...."
The musicians were attuned to her every nuance and impulse and led us into singing *How Great Thou Art.*

All over the auditorium people were raising their hands as they sang. There was freedom. Freedom to pour out one's heart to the Creator. Freedom to thank the Saviour. Freedom to receive the Holy Spirit.

I was aware that the handsome young Mexican on my left with the rich baritone voice was no longer singing in English. He had shifted into Spanish—worshiping God in his native tongue—and his eyes were sparkling as his voice blended with the thousands of others.

Then Miss Kuhlman spoke. She called for a moment of silent prayer. The organ underscored her words with soft music as the chimes were sounded. "There is power in the name of Jesus," she said softly into the microphone. As she spoke, a deep, holy hush settled over the immense congregation, broken here and there by soft, muted exclamations of "Dear Jesus," and "Praise God."

She continued: "We know, Father, that miracles are going to happen in this place today. We feel the blessed presence of the Holy Spirit. We promise to give You all the praise, all the glory, for what is about to happen here. Pour out Your Spirit upon us, for Jesus' sake...."

After the prayer, she became folksy. Extending a friendly greeting to the congregation, she asked, "Where are you from? Shout it out." A quick poll revealed that nearly every state in the Union was represented as well as Japan, Finland, Holland, Brazil, Jamaica, New Zealand, India, Arabia, Panama, Greece, Germany, France....

"France?" she laughed. "I wish you would go back and bring Mr. DeGaulle with you." Everybody laughed. "You know," she continued, "if the United Nations would meet in the name of Jesus like we are doing, there would be no more wars." The crowd applauded.

That is another thing I discovered about the miracle service. It pulsates with laughter. Kathryn Kuhlman does not believe in a gloomy religion. At times her sense of humor reveals a quiet, wry wit that brings a ripple of smiles to the surface of the lake of people in front of her. At other times she is comical and jocular, almost uproariously funny. But it is all spontaneous. She never tells jokes.

"Say," she said, "the most wonderful thing has happened." She paused for effect. "I have just discovered that three young men from the carrier *Enterprise* have flown up from San Diego just to be in this service. Where are you fellows? Wherever you are, come up here to the platform. We want to honor you."

From three separate points in the massive congregation, three handsome young naval airmen converged on the platform. They were obviously embarrassed by this unexpected recognition and stood with shy smiles while Miss Kuhlman motioned them to come closer to the microphone.

"These men are responsible for you being here. If it were not for them, and thousands like them who are willing to risk their lives to defend this great nation of ours, none of us could gather in freedom today. And I want to go on record saying I am proud of our men in the armed forces...." She was interrupted and finally drowned out by the roar of applause from the audience.

She walked toward the three men and placed her hands on their heads to pray for them. Immediately, two of her ushers broke from the wings and rushed to where they were standing. They know from past experience that when Miss Kuhlman prays for people in circumstances such as this, the power of God falls in such a mysterious way that those being prayed for simply crumple to the floor. Sure enough, as she began to pray for them, the young men crumpled backward. Caught by the diligent ushers, they were laid gently on the floor.*

A great gasp went up from the congregation and Kathryn Kuhlman turned and walked back toward the center of the stage, shaking her head and holding her hands in the air. She seemed utterly amazed at the power of God.

I was watching the expression on the face of a young ophthalmologist from UCLA, a guest on the platform as an observer. He had told me earlier that he was thrilled by the genuine healings he had witnessed in another meeting, but was still confused by this falling under the power. He glanced at me across the platform and our eyes met. He shook his head and shrugged his shoulders in dismay. (In less than twenty minutes, that same young doctor would be stretched full length on the floor having gone under the power when Miss Kuhlman prayed for him.)

Again, Miss Kuhlman addressed the audience. "Let me tell you what happened several weeks ago in Pittsburgh. I wish you could meet my new friend, Gordon Wilson. He was in the miracle service that day and had

---

*The phenomenon of persons crumpling when Miss Kuhlman lays hands on them or prays for them has characterized her ministry since its inception. She readily admits she has no explanation for it except to say that it is the power of the Holy Spirit. To back this up, she quotes Scripture: Acts 9 tells of Saul having a face-to-face encounter with the Spirit of Christ and falling to the ground on the Damascus Road; Matthew 17 relates the story of the three apostles on the Mount of Transfiguration who could not stand to their feet in the presence of God. Further investigation shows that this same phenomenon accompanied many of the great evangelists in history such as Charles G. Finney, Peter Cartwright, and Dwight L. Moody. "Falling under the power" was also quite prevalent in some of the world's great revivals and at the Great Awakening (1740-55) with George Whitefield and the Welsh Revival (1904) with Evan Roberts.

driven all the way from a tiny little town eighty miles west of Ottawa in Canada. And not only that, he had brought four women with him, all of them crippled and one of them in a wheel chair.

"Not only was this man healed of bleeding ulcers, but everyone in that car received a healing blessing—and one of the ladies was the wife of one of the two doctors in that little Canadian village."

There was a stirring in the congregation and I could hear people saying, "Praise God" and "Hallelujah."

"But wait," Miss Kuhlman continued, her voice more intense but still quiet. "That is not the most amazing thing. The amazing thing is that Mr. Wilson went back to Ontario, chartered a bus and brought the whole bus load of people the next week. And since then it seems like half the population of that precious little town has been to Pittsburgh for a miracle service." The crowd joined in laughter and applause.

"But Pittsburgh is not the only place where people are healed," she continued and the crowd murmured its approval. "Today, I want you to meet someone very special to me...just to show you that those who get healed stay healed."

A sweet-faced woman in a dark blue dress walked onto the platform holding aloft a pair of crutches. Her face beamed. "You tell them what happened, honey," Miss Kuhlman said.

"When I came to the service last month, I could not walk without crutches," she said, her voice clear but trembling with emotion. "I had surgery twelve times on one foot and fifteen times on the other. They had removed the metatarsal heads, the balls of the feet, and the other bones, too. The soles were then rebuilt with flesh taken from my stomach."

"You mean you were walking on your stomach?" Miss Kuhlman asked, laughing.

"Well, yes, but not without the crutches. I could hardly bear to touch the floor, the pain was so bad. Now I can do this." The woman stomped her foot on the floor—hard. The congregation applauded.

Miss Kuhlman turned to a distinguished looking man standing on the platform behind her. "Dr. Biery," she said, "you examined this lady last month during the service. As a medical doctor, what do you say about this?"

Dr. Martin L. Biery, a specialist in General Surgery for thirty years, with degrees in medicine from the University of Michigan and Michigan State University, walked to the microphone.

"When I examined this lady I found that, just as she said, virtually all the bones in her feet were missing. This made normal walking impossible and there should be great pain and tenderness. But when I examined her after her healing, there was no pain or tenderness at all. If it were simply a remission and not a healing, the pain should have returned by today."

"Show us that you can walk," Miss Kuhlman instructed. The woman walked back across the platform, deliberately stomping her feet at intervals. "What do you say to that, Dr. Biery?" said Miss Kuhlman.

"That," he replied, "has to come from God."

"Yes, that has to come from God," Miss Kuhlman said softly. Then she lifted her eyes and prayed, "Dear Jesus, all we can say is thank You—thanks a million."

At this point, the lady who had been healed was weeping. Dr. Biery was weeping. Miss Kuhlman was weeping. And I, too, was wiping my eyes with my handkerchief.

The next moment we were laughing as Miss Kuhlman described an incident that took place a short time before in Pittsburgh. "Unknown to me, we had a Catholic priest from New York in our miracle service. Something happened to him during that service—something wonderful. This is how he expressed it in a letter to me:

> Dear Miss Kuhlman,
>
> All praise to the Eternal Father. All praise to Jesus Christ. All praise to the Holy Spirit, for the Spirit has come to me. I wept as I have never wept, and laughed as I have never laughed, and praised as I have never praised, and cried out as I have never cried out—all this in my car this morning on the way home....

"A short time later," she continued, "he wrote again, inviting me to hold services in his town. He said, 'I am sorry that it is not possible for me to invite you to preach in my church. But if you will come, I will rent the auditorium for you. I will back you to the hilt that others might experience what I have experienced.'"

Miss Kuhlman added with a touch of jest, "This reminds me of the little Catholic girl who came to the miracle service with her mother and said, 'Oh, Mommy, wouldn't Miss Kuhlman make a wonderful Father!'"

Then she grew very serious. Her voice was low and husky; she was almost whispering. "There is a beautiful presence of the Holy Spirit here today. It must have been something like this in the early church when the Holy Spirit began to descend upon those early Christians as they gathered to worship.

"The light of God's love is in this place. But it is dark outside, and it is getting darker. There is so much hate out there, so much greed out there, so much misunderstanding out there. And the only hope is the love of God.

"That is why you are here today—to see the love and the power of God at work in this place. You would not walk across the street to see Kathryn Kuhlman, I know that. I cannot preach. I cannot sing. I can only love you."

Tears were running down her cheeks and most of us were wet-eyed, too. Yet there was no hysteria. Our hearts were being genuinely touched and moved, but the emotion was too deep for noise. She was whispering now. "I love God with every atom of my being. And I know that in this place today the Holy Spirit is moving gently...gently...."

Every eye was fixed on that lone figure in the center of the stage. Every ear strained to catch the incandescent words. Even the coughing and movement in the seats had stopped.

"Over here," she said suddenly, pointing to a spot under the balcony. "Somewhere over here someone has just received a healing for asthma. I do not know who you are, but you came to this service wheezing with asthma and it has just disappeared. The Spirit bears witness to my spirit that you have just been healed."

The congregation now came alive with an expectant rustling.

"Somebody's ear has just opened. It happened not more than a minute ago." (Miss Kuhlman cannot explain how she knows the persons and the illnesses of which they are healed. But she does. And the ushers and workers know that when she reports a healing, there has been a healing. "I know these things," she says, "but I do not pretend to understand why or how I know."

There was a great deal of movement in the congregation as people began to rise to their feet to claim healings.

"Diabetes is being healed. To my right, in the first balcony, somebody is being healed of diabetes. Don't be frightened, that heat in your body right now is supernatural.

"And a growth—a tumor—has disappeared from the back of someone's neck. A person up there in the second balcony. Feel the back of your neck and you will find that the growth is gone.

"An extreme case of sinus is instantly healed. You had some kind of operation on your nose in the last two months, but it did not help. Now that sinus is completely healed.

"There is a heart being healed. A man with a heart that was more than half dead has just been healed.

"A blind eye is clearing and vision is being restored right now as I speak. Up there, in the balcony to my left.

"And there is a man, an elderly man, down here some place," she gestured to her left, "who is being healed of a painful prostate gland. That operation will not be necessary, God has taken care of it right now.

"Oh, there is so much power here today," she exclaimed, "it is everywhere. The power of God is everywhere. It is so strong I can hardly keep on my feet."

A large group of people had gathered on both sides of the stage to testify of their healings. An usher announced that the first woman in line was the one with asthma whom Miss Kuhlman had mentioned. Others testified they had been sitting just where Miss Kuhlman indicated and had been healed of the exact disease she described.

"What is this? What is this?" she exclaimed as one of her staff members escorted a young woman in stocking feet to the front of the line. The woman was weeping profusely.

The staff member, a tall, dignified woman, stepped to the microphone. "Miss Kuhlman, this woman has been in a wheelchair for two years. She came to the service in a wheelchair, but look at her now."

"In a wheelchair!" Miss Kuhlman exclaimed, having difficulty accepting the enormity of the miracle herself. "This is the first time I have seen her. She was healed and no one knew it but the Holy Spirit. Tell me, honey, where do you go to church?"

"I am a Southern Baptist," the woman choked out between sobs.

"A Baptist, and a Southern one at that. If God can heal a Baptist, He can heal anybody." A wave of soft laughter ran through the congregation.

This was another thing I was discovering about those who were healed. There seemed to be no set pattern. And surprisingly enough, most of those healed came from main line church denominations rather than from the Pentecostal branches. And Catholics, Jews, even agnostics, receive the blessings of God along with the fundamental Christians. Miss Kuhlman unhesitatingly points out the prophecy, "...In the last days, saith God, I will pour out my Spirit upon all flesh..." (Acts 2:17).

Miss Kuhlman, still quizzing the young woman who had walked away from her wheelchair, asked, "Is your husband here?" The woman nodded and pointed somewhere in the auditorium. "Well, call him up here," Miss Kuhlman said, laughing.

"Rob—ert!" she wailed into the microphone.

A man hurried down the aisle. He took the stage steps three at a time and enveloped his wife in his arms, lifting her completely off the floor as he buried his head in her shoulder. Both were weeping openly, and Miss Kuhlman stepped back as the joyful drama unfolded before our eyes.

Dr. Robert Hoyt, a professor of pathology, was seated beside me on the stage. He turned and whispered, "Now do you see why I support this ministry? I would not miss one of these services for anything in the world." Too emotionally choked to answer, I nodded in agreement.

"Bring her wheelchair," Miss Kuhlman said. With a flash of humor, she made the husband sit in the wheelchair and had the young woman push him off the stage. The congregation roared their approval.

A young woman from Arabia was brought to the microphone by an usher. "Miss Kuhlman, this young woman came to America to receive surgery on her eye. She came to the service on the invitation of a friend before entering the hospital tomorrow. Now her vision is perfect."

"Is this correct?" Miss Kuhlman asked the pretty, dark-skinned young lady.

"That is right," the girl replied with a heavy accent, laboring over her choice of words. "I had blood clot on the optic nerve, but now I see perfectly. I do not understand. What has happened?"

Miss Kuhlman asked another physician on the platform, a woman, Dr. Viola Frymann, from La Jolla, California, to examine the woman. Dr. Frymann made a quick examination of the woman's eye and then stepped back, holding up fingers and asking her to count them.

"This woman's vision is now apparently normal," Dr. Frymann reported to the congregation. "Under normal circumstances, a blood clot on the optic nerve would not clear."

A middle-aged man from Washington State testified that a back infection had eaten out one of the vertebrae in his spine and he had a disc removed three months before. He said he was in severe pain when the service started but was instantly healed at the very moment Miss Kuhlman said a man with a spinal condition was being healed. He demonstrated he was now able to bend and stretch in all directions with ease.

Dr. Biery commented: "What this man has just experienced is medically impossible. When a disc has been recently removed, any motion causes extreme pain. This must be God."

An elderly man stepped in front of the microphone, obviously trying to contain his emotion. "My throat," he said," "I have not been able to swallow without extreme pain for thirty years. Now I am healed."

"When did this happen?" Miss Kuhlman asked.

"Over an hour ago," the man confessed. "But I was afraid to say anything for fear the pain would return. But it is all gone and I can talk and swallow without any pain at all."

"What do you do for a living?" Miss Kuhlman asked.

"I am retired now," he said, still trembling with emotion, "but I was a practicing physician for more than forty years."

A young housewife was next in line. She was weeping. "What is it?" asked Miss Kuhlman.

"I need to give up smoking," she sobbed.

"Smoking?" Miss Kuhlman said in amazement. "I have said nothing about smoking. I never preach on smoking. Yet you want to give it up. Why?'

"Because I want to be clean," the woman said. "But I cannot stop." She fumbled in her small purse and pulled out a crumpled pack of cigarettes and laid them on the speaker's stand.

"Do not put those things up there," Miss Kuhlman said. "Throw them on the floor where they belong. God is going to remove all desire from you right now."

She put both hands on the woman's head and began to pray. "Dear Jesus, so fill this precious one with Your *pray* love and power that she will never need another cigarette...." The woman's knees buckled and she collapsed to the floor.

And so it went on.

"This man is a Methodist minister," Miss Kuhlman announced, indicating a well-dressed man of middle age standing on the platform beside her. "He had the courage to come up here and say, 'Miss Kuhlman, I do not have the power of the Holy Spirit in my life and ministry. Please pray that I will.'" She began to pray and instantly he collapsed to the floor.

"That is the power of God," Miss Kuhlman said. "I have nothing to do with this whatsoever; this is the power of the Holy Spirit. If there are other ministers here today who want more of the Spirit in their ministries, come forward now."

Immediately, men began moving out of their seats and heading for the platform. Some were in business suits, others wore clerical garb. Many had been sitting in the congregation incognito, afraid to identify themselves as ministers, but now were willing to do so to receive the power of God. Soon the platform was filled with clergymen.

There were Episcopalian rectors, Presbyterian pastors, ministers who unashamedly acknowledged their need for a deeper spiritual experience and their hunger for a greater manifestation of God's power in their own ministry—completely oblivious to the fact that members of their own congregation were out there in the audience. It was a sight and experience never to be forgotten. Miss Kuhlman prayed for each of them.

A young woman was next in line and spoke quietly to Miss Kuhlman. "This young lady is a college professor from Texas and she says she wants to be saved...to be born again," Miss Kuhlman said to the crowd. "Healing is marvelous, but the greatest miracle is the transformation of a soul from darkness to light. I do not care if I never see another body healed, as long as I know that there are souls being saved. Healing of the body is nothing compared to the healing of the soul."

Miss Kuhlman moved toward the young woman and touched her gently with her hand. "Dear Jesus, forgive *pray* her sin and baptize her with the Holy Ghost." There was an audible gasp from the congregation as the woman's legs slowly buckled and she fell backward. An usher caught her and gently lowered her to the floor where she lay with arms stretched heavenward and her lips softly uttering a strange, melodic language.

"I believe in speaking in tongues when it is like this, don't you?" Miss Kuhlman asked. The congregation murmured its approval, still awestruck by what was transpiring on the stage.

It was almost five o'clock at the Shrine. The service has been in process for more than three hours and I could see that many people were standing in the vestibule and on the front steps, craning their necks to see inside the packed auditorium. The month before, I had learned, more than three thousand had been turned away for lack of seats.

I sensed that Miss Kuhlman was deliberately pointing the service towards a climax. We were approaching that part which she considers the most important aspect of her ministry.

"I believe that the blood of Jesus Christ is sufficient atonement for sin," she declared in ringing tones. "The healing of the body, as marvelous as it is, is secondary to the healing of the soul. If you have never been born again, if you have never tasted the joy of salvation, if you have never made a total commitment of your life to God's Son, Jesus Christ, I want you to do it right now. Jesus said, 'Him that cometh to me I will in no wise cast out.'"

And they came. The organ broke into a refrain as the aisles filled with people. By the score, they streamed down the aisles from every part of the huge auditorium. The elderly, the middle aged, teenagers—all were coming.

Some were in tears. Others had shining faces, as though they had already experienced salvation even as they walked down the aisles. Some walked quickly, their jaws set as though afraid that if they hesitated they might change their minds. Others plodded, seemingly weighed down by heavy burdens.

They filled the platform and clogged the steps and aisles approaching the stage. They crowded in, trying to get close enough to Miss Kuhlman that she could put her hands on them and pray. Faces were eager and straining, surging forward, trying to get close enough to be touched in prayer.

"We could not possibly pronounce a benediction on a service such as this," Miss Kuhlman said to those who remained in their seats (and it seemed that at least half of the congregation had come forward and was standing around the stage). "All I can say is as you go, rejoice at the marvelous things God has done in this place today."

The mighty organ boomed, the choir broke into a spirited rendition of *He's the Saviour of My Soul,* and Miss Kuhlman turned to walk off stage. She moved among the wheelchairs of those who had not been healed, praying for first one and then another. She laid her hands on the inert bodies that lay upon the stretchers and she prayed for tiny children being held out by the straining arms of anxious parents.

The crowd in the great auditorium turned to leave, but theirs was a reluctant departure. Some remained standing in their places, their faces lifted to God, enthralled in prayer. Others, perfect strangers, were exchanging greetings.

An old man who had been healed of a spinal deformity was standing in the aisle looking around in awe and wonder. "Isn't it wonderful!" he said to me as I passed up the aisle.

"What do you mean?" I inquired.

"The love! You can just feel it in this place, can't you?" He kept looking around in wonder.

And he was right. As someone remarked, "Kathryn Kuhlman is not a faith healer. She is a love healer."

As I wandered out from the great auditorium, still supercharged with the power of God, I kept asking myself, Where have I been all my life? I thought of the years I had spent in churches where people scorned the idea that God is dead—yet acted as if they were at His funeral every Sunday. Dozens of names flashed through my mind—sick friends, ministers, fellow Christians, skeptics, loved ones. How I wished they could have shared this experience with me.

My life will never be the same.

Jamie Buckingham

21

2

God Always Answers Little Girls' Prayers

(A Skeptic is Healed)
by Fred Burdick

Fred Burdick is a building contractor in Foster City, California. He and his wife, Fran, live in one of the nation's first model cities, just south of San Francisco. He was twenty-three years of age and the father of two small girls when he had a disabling accident.

"Mama, how many more sleeps before Daddy is healed?" Every night for a week, Maria, age six, and Lisa, age five, would ask their mother the same question. They were so sure that God was going to heal their daddy; and that daddy tells exactly what happened.

It was a gray, chilly afternoon. We had almost completed the four-story building and were ready to put the roof into place. I was standing on a small ledge four floors above the street directing my construction crew in placing a pre-fab roof. The huge crane was swinging one of the two hundred pound sections into place so my men could juggle it into final position.

Moving along the high ledge above the street, I bent over to nail a truss in place. Suddenly and without warning, the heavy roof section slipped from the high crane and smashed across the small of my back. I teetered on the ledge and then fell forward through a ceiling joist onto the concrete floor of the unfinished fourth story. The roof section glanced off the ledge and crashed to the ground almost forty feet below.

I knew I was seriously injured. The construction foreman was close by, but I was in a state of shock and he had to wait for others to arrive before they could get me to my feet. Waves of dizziness and nausea swept over me as the men lowered me down an inside ladder to the ground.

I was rushed to a doctor, but his examination did not determine the extent of my injury. I was only twenty-three years old, and I felt I ought to be able to return to work. But I was wrong.

The pain increased and five days later I was back at the doctor's office for X-rays and tests. He immediately admitted me to Sequoia Hospital in Redwood City for a thorough examination.

There, the doctors tried to explain what had happened. "Mr. Burdick, many of the muscles and tendons have been ripped loose in your spinal column. This is causing extreme pressure on some of the nerves. Our tests show paralysis in your legs which will grow worse unless we begin treatment." The pain was agonizing and I readily agreed to the treatment.

The next three weeks I lay in traction with heavy weights attached to my legs. The only time the weights were removed was when I was taken to therapy where they treated me with massage, heat, and hot water baths.

I showed improvement and the doctors released me to return to work on a limited basis. "No lifting or prolonged bending," they warned. They didn't have to worry. The ever-present pain was reminder enough.

But in only a matter of days the pain became so acute I had to return to the hospital. This time, they were giving me shots of codeine every four hours to ease the pain. And they resumed the traction and therapy.

The days grew longer as my body was spread out with heavy weights attached to my legs, stretching the muscles in my spine to relieve the pressure on the nerves. When I was released, the doctor gave my wife Fran instructions to continue the treatment at home with massage, heat packs, and the constant use of drugs. I didn't realize it at the time, but I was slowly becoming dependent on the codeine that was a part of my everyday routine.

The insurance adjustor suggested that I should collect damages from the company for time lost from work and medical payments. He talked with my doctors and they declared me sixty-three percent permanently disabled. This shocked me, for up until this time I had felt that I was going to get well. The horrible realization that at such an early age I was doomed to be a semi-invalid was more than my emotional system could stand. I began to crack.

But there was nothing that could be done. "We could operate," the doctors said, "but our tests show there is an eighty percent chance you will be permanently paralyzed if we do."

"Anything is better than this," I told them, "the pain is unbearable and I cannot function anyway. Please, please do something." But "wait" was all they said.

25

My lawyer filed suit. The Industrial Accident Commission granted a temporary settlement for the loss of my legs and the prospect of a life of acute pain.

By this time I could only walk with a cane. The days stretched into months and the months into years. The pain got steadily worse until I felt I could take no more. The hospitalizations became more frequent and I grew more and more dependent on the increasing dosage of drugs.

Our home life was a shambles. Poor Fran; she tried so hard to be patient with me. But after a long hospitalization I would return to the house and expect her to maintain the same routine I had in the hospital—not taking into account that she had two little girls and a house to take care of...plus a crabby, demanding, pain-ridden husband. On the long days when all I could do was stagger from the bed to the sofa and shout for my drugs, she sometimes gave up. I would hear her back in the bathroom, with the door closed, crying in frustration and despair.

We had a beautiful home, one I had built myself. But it became a prison to me. I cursed the sunken living room that meant I had to climb two steps to get to the kitchen or the bathroom.

My little girls, Maria and Lisa, would plead with me to play with them, but I couldn't even hold them on my knee, much less pick them up.

Time and time again I would fall and be unable to get up. My neighbor said that every time he saw little Maria running across the street, he knew he would have to come help me up off the floor. I was growing desperate and discouraged.

We went from one doctor to another, but all told us the same thing. The muscles and ligaments had been ripped loose and when they grew back, they had pinched the nerves. Any muscle pressure or exercise caused extreme pain and sometimes instant paralysis.

The nights were worse than the days. When I slept, Fran said I would groan from the pain all night. Many nights I stayed awake, shuffling through the dark house on my cane, trying to find relief.

The drugs were helping less and less and on at least one occasion, I got drunk trying to kill the pain. I didn't know (and at that point didn't care anyway) that the mixture of alcohol and drugs could have killed me. Only a heavy meal earlier in the evening, which absorbed the pill, saved my life.

I guess most people would have turned to God as a last resort. But I was a religious rebel. I had been forced against my will earlier in life and was now rebelling against anything spiritual. I scoffed, even in my pain, at those who said they were going to pray for me. I was a rough, tough construction boss and had no use for the panty-waists and sissies who believed in God. That was for weaklings. I could stand alone.

But I wasn't standing alone. I was leaning on the drugs. "We've got to pull you off the codeine, Fred," my doctor said. "The last blood tests showed you are at the addiction point."

I pleaded with him to let me have the pills. "I don't care if I am an addict," I argued. "What's the difference? I'm hopeless anyway." He agreed to let me continue—out of sheer pity, I think. Only God and Fran knew how much I suffered, but Fran was the only one I ever complained to.

Then, in December 1966, Fran had an operation. By the time she got home from the hospital, I was a physical and emotional wreck. That first evening, still weak from her surgery, she fixed supper and began to clean up the kitchen. I never tried to walk from the kitchen into the living room alone because of those two steps, but that evening I staggered out of the kitchen to watch TV. I never made it.

As I started down the step, my leg collapsed. It just gave way without warning and I pitched forward on the living room floor where I twisted in horrible pain.

Maria screamed for her mother. Fran stood on the top step with her hand to her mouth trying to stifle a scream. She ran to me but was unable to get me on my feet. I'd never experienced such intense pain.

I heard her fumbling with the phone trying to call our neighbor, but her mind had gone blank in hysteria and she couldn't remember the number. The door slammed shut behind her as she stumbled across the street in the dark screaming for help.

Our neighbor and his three boys rushed over and got me on the sofa. I was in a cold sweat, shaking and screaming in pain every time I was moved. Fran called the doctor and he recognized her voice from the many, many calls before. "Get him to the hospital as soon as you can," he said.

This time, I was to remain there seven weeks.

Christmas Eve came and the doctor gave me a twenty-four hour pass. "Walk slowly and climb no steps," he cautioned, "or they may be the last steps you will ever climb."

We celebrated Christmas Eve at my mother's house—in the garage, so I would not have to climb the steps to get into the house. The next day, Christmas, Fran had to call off her big dinner to take me back to the hospital early. I had fallen on my way to the table and couldn't get back to my feet. The children cried the rest of the day, Fran later told me.

When I was finally released from the hospital the last of February, the doctor fitted me with an awkward brace that hung across my shoulders and laced tight around my waist and hips. But I was developing huge calcium deposits on my spine and they made the brace almost impossible to wear. The doctor said surgery was the only way they could be removed.

While in the hospital I had received a shot of Demerol every four hours. But now that I was home, I turned to the pills for relief. I couldn't seem to get enough. I was hooked. I was a drug addict. But the pain was so constant and so intense, I just didn't care. It looked like the end of the world.

While I was in the hospital, something different had been happening at home. My wife and our neighbor's wife had been listening to Kathryn Kuhlman's radio broadcast over KFAX in San Francisco. The neighbor then gave Fran a copy of *I Believe in Miracles* and asked their minister to visit me in the hospital.

Fran's life was changing. She had been reared a Roman Catholic, but never had worked at it very hard. Now her faith in God was coming to life like a sprig of grass that suddenly finds a crack in the bottom side of a rock and inches upward toward the sunlight.

When I got home, Fran felt we should return the minister's kindness and attend one of his church services. We were both deeply impressed with the friendliness and hospitality of the people. Several weeks later we joined the church.

Things were beginning to happen. Fran, who was getting more and more excited over Kathryn Kuhlman, learned that Miss Kuhlman was going to be speaking at a luncheon in downtown San Francisco. All the tickets had been sold, but on the day before the luncheon our neighbor, who had a ticket, got sick, and gave the ticket to Fran.

She came back home the next afternoon bubbling with enthusiasm. "People were healed! I saw it!" she exclaimed. "I talked with a woman who was healed of a back injury. Fred, I just know it can happen to you. Miss Kuhlman's going to be back in San Francisco in six weeks at Memorial Temple on Nob Hill. You're going to be healed in that meeting."

"Either you have lost your mind or got drunk at that luncheon," I snorted. She was drunk all right, but I knew nothing about the "new wine" at the time.

I began to be bombarded with prayer. People from the church visited and said they were praying for me. I was polite, but inwardly I sneered at their ignorance. I later learned that some of them were fasting and staying up all night praying for me.

Fran chided me. "You ought to be ashamed. These people have sore knees from praying, and all you do is scoff and sneer." She was right, but I was resigned to a life of pain.

My lawyer said we ought to continue the lawsuit against the company since I had grown so much worse. "We've got a good case, Fred," he assured me. "I think we can sue for a substantial amount and collect it." I agreed.

Fran had other plans. She was determined that I was going to be healed in the Kathryn Kuhlman service. "You're wasting your time," I told her. But she kept right on.

She would try to read to me from Miss Kuhlman's book. "Listen to this," she'd say as she began to read aloud. "Isn't it wonderful!" she'd remark, with tears running down her face as she read of one miracle after another.

"I'm more dumbfounded by your crying than I am by those silly fairy stories," I said.

"Go ahead and be a skeptic. God's going to heal you anyway." She had also told Maria and Lisa that God was going to heal me and they began to pray for me in their nightly prayers.

One afternoon, Fran was reading the book when the girls frolicked through the room and pulled it out of her hands. "Now I've lost my place," Fran scolded them. As she opened the book to try to find her place again, her eyes fell on a single sentence: "God always hears the prayers of little girls."

That did it! From then on, nothing could sway her from the conviction that I was going to be healed.

"It's all a bunch of baloney," I said. "No intelligent man will buy that stuff about healings." But Fran kept right on believing. She even made a reservation on the bus to take us from our area to the meeting.

I made an appointment with a new neurosurgeon to enter the hospital for a new series of tests on the same weekend Fran had resolved I was to attend the services. By this time, I was pleading with them to operate, even if it meant I would be paralyzed. I would do anything to stop the pain.

"Fred, please put it off for a week," Fran pleaded. "You've just got to attend the Kathryn Kuhlman service. Can't you get the doctor to wait for a week? You can go in Monday after the service if you want. Please put it off."

"The doctor will think I am crazy," I said. "You cannot arrange these things at your own convenience. He has to do it."

She pleaded further. She threatened. She cried. She screamed. She used every tactic known to woman to get me to change my mind and attend the service. "Fran, you don't understand. The insurance company has already spent $28,000 in medical bills. Now they have agreed to this. I can't call if off."

But I did. There was no other way to keep my sanity in the face of her determination. It is a decision I will thank God for the rest of my life.

The following Sunday, we boarded the oldest, most dilapidated piece of junk I'd ever seen. "This is a bus?" I asked sarcastically as we sat down on the torn cushions.

"I'm sorry, honey," she said. "But it will be worth it. You will see."

As we bounced down the rough roads, I had the distinct impression that all the springs and shock absorbers had been removed. The seats seemed to be fastened to the axle and every jar sent waves of pain up and down my spine. I glared at Fran. "That driver's hitting every hole on purpose!"

"Fred," she said as a tear ran down her cheek, "if I didn't know for a fact that you were going to be healed this afternoon, I'd ask him to let us off right now. But I know...I just know you are going to be healed."

"How do you know?" I snarled between gasps of pain. "What makes you so sure?"

"I don't know. I just trust in God and feel that He wants you healed. I've been praying for this so long and so have the children. And, you know, Miss Kuhlman says God always answers the prayers of little girls. I have even prayed you would be healed early in the service so I could enjoy the rest of it."

I sat silently, stewing in my own anger and pain, as the old bus jarred along. Fran spoke again, choosing her words slowly. "Fred, I am so confident that you are going to be healed that I asked your mother to keep the girls tonight so we can go out and celebrate."

"You what?" I exploded. Her nagging had been bad enough, but this was more than I could take. She just hung her head and I could see her lips moving in silent prayer.

"What's the use?" I thought. "I'm trapped. I might as well make the best of it. But I'll never get caught in a mess like this again."

If only I could have seen an hour into the future. If only I could have known what God had in store for me. But I was bound by little knowledge and less faith and therefore trapped in my self-made prison of pride and self-pity.

The bus arrived just as the doors of the auditorium swung open. By the time I got off, every seat in the lower section was filled. A friend of Fran's helped her get me up the long flight of stairs to the top balcony. Another friend, a member of our church, saw us coming and gave up his seat. I gingerly lowered myself down, wincing from the pain. Fran stood, leaning against the wall in the aisle beside me.

The choir had just finished singing when Miss Kuhlman appeared on stage. She was dressed in a brilliant pink dress and waved at the audience as they applauded. Then she broke into song, motioning the congregation to join in. Everyone around me was singing—everyone but me, that is.

"Who does she think she is?" I muttered to myself. "A woman preacher! Boy, I must be the biggest nut in the world to get caught up in something like this."

As the service progressed, people began going up to the stage saying they had been healed. What kind of magic was this? Surely all of these people couldn't be fakes?

Just then Miss Kuhlman stopped and pointed toward the balcony. "There's a young man in the balcony who has just been healed of a serious spine injury. He is some place in the top balcony. I do not know who he is or what his problem is, but he's just been healed of a spinal injury. Stand up. Stand up and accept your healing."

Fran started poking me. "Fred! Fred! That's it. She's talking about you. Stand up. Stand up!"

I looked around. Some of the people were looking at me. I was embarrassed and refused to budge. "Fred, God is healing you. Stand up and accept it."

I shook my head and tried to slip down as far as I could in the seat. But one of Miss Kuhlman's workers came up the aisle and leaned down over me. "I think Miss Kuhlman is talking about you. Don't you have a spinal injury?" I just gave her a blank look. "Why don't you trust Jesus and stand to your feet?" she asked.

I wanted to shake my head, but some strange, mysterious power was forcing me to my feet. I reached for the sides of the chair to pull myself up, but realized I didn't need the support of my arms any more. I could stand alone. And the pain—the pain was gone.

I stretched forward and slowly began to twist back and forth. The worker asked me to step into the aisle and to stretch in different directions. I could hardly believe it. The pain was gone. My back was limber and pliable.

I turned to say something to Fran, but she was crying. "Oh, Fred, praise God. Praise God! Praise God!" That was all she could say.

It was unbelievable! I hadn't prayed. I hadn't had an ounce of faith. I had scoffed and scorned what was taking place. And yet, suddenly and without reason, I had been miraculously healed.

"Walk back and forth up the aisle," the worker suggested. I did more than that. I began to run. Down the aisle and then back up. The people in the balcony were looking at me. Some of them had their hands up praising God. I didn't care. I was healed.

The worker said, "Would you like to go to the platform with me?"

I didn't wait for her, but started down the steps. I was running. When I got to the bottom, I turned and ran back up, three at a time. It was real! Even the jar and shock of my feet hitting the floor in a dead run caused no pain. I ran back down, bouncing and jogging to test my back. It was as though I had never been hurt; no pain, no soreness, not even any stiffness.

We approached the platform and Miss Kuhlman saw me coming and reached out her hand. "What is your name, young man? Have you been healed?"

I had never been able to speak in public, but that afternoon I stood before those thousands of people and told them what had happened to me. They broke into spontaneous applause. All over the auditorium, I could hear people praising God. I found myself saying it, "Praise God! Thank You, Jesus! Thank You!" And before I knew it, I was under the power of God, stretched out full length on the floor. Me—the skeptic—healed!

Fran and I did celebrate that night. And what a celebration. There had never been two happier people in all the world.

Afterwards, we went back to my mother's to pick up the girls. For the first time in three years I was able to pick them up. "Fred, your back!" my mother screamed. I just laughed. I felt stronger than I had in all my life.

About a year before, while I was still working part-time, I had caught my right thumb between a truck and a heavy plank. The thumb had been crushed from the knuckle down and all the flesh and tissue had been stripped, leaving only the exposed bone tip. The doctors had fashioned a thumb tip out of liquid silicone and attached it to the stub. They then grafted skin around it from my forearm.

"It's just an ornament," they said. "Of course it will never be movable or have feeling because it's not alive."

That night, Maria and Lisa asked me, "Daddy, did God heal your thumb, too?"

I grinned and said, "No, angels, God was too busy healing my back."

"But we prayed for your thumb, too," they said with obvious disappointment. "We believed God would answer that prayer, too."

I tousled their heads with my hand. "Well, I think one healing is enough, don't you? Besides, this thumb is only artificial. You don't think God could bring it to life, do you?" But I had a strong feeling that they believed just that.

We decided to ride with some friends to the church to testify about my healing. The Sunday night services would still be in process. On the way across town I suddenly noticed a strange tingling in my right hand. I look down. My thumb was twitching and I could move it. There was feeling in it—there was life in it.

"Oh, Daddy," the girls sang out. "God did answer our prayer, didn't He?" He did indeed!

Two days later, all the calcium deposits had disappeared from my backbone. The swelling and knots were completely gone. I was ready for anything by then. The next day I called my lawyer. "You can call off the lawsuit," I told him. "I've been healed."

"What?" he shouted into the phone. "Is this some kind of a joke or something?"

"No," I assured him. "I've been healed. My back is well."

"Wait! Don't say another word. Come to my office immediately and we'll talk in private. But don't tell a single person about this." I agreed, but I did not have the heart to tell him that I had already told several thousand people about it the day before.

He tried to convince me that it was a psychosomatic remission. "Take a couple of weeks and get away," he urged. "When things get back to normal, the pain will return and we can continue on with the case."

"It's no use. My back is healed."

"It can't be," he cried. "Backs just don't get well overnight." I left him in a state of shock. He kept saying over and over, "Take things easy for a few weeks and you will be back to normal."

But I had been in pain for three years and did not want that kind of normalcy. I was healed and that is something that money cannot buy.

The next week Fran and I took our first outdoor excursion in three years. We drove up to Lake Tahoe for a skiing retreat. I had always loved to ski, but we had resigned ourselves to the belief that we would never be able to go again.

Fran and some friends (the ones who had been praying so hard for me) stayed on top of a hill while I sat in an inner tube and scooted down the incline on the seat of my pants. I was going at a terrific rate of speed when

I hit a bump, catapulted into the air and came down head first against a tree.

As I clambered to my feet and shook the snow out of my ears, I heard Fran shout from the top of the hill, "Praise the Lord!"

I chuckled and said to myself, as I gasped for breath, "Amen!"

Three weeks later, when I next put on my suit coat to go to church, I felt something in the pocket. I had forgotten about the pills, the narcotics. They had never crossed my mind all this time. I had carried them to the meeting on Nob Hill, certain I would need them before the afternoon was over. But the healing was total and complete. I knew I would never need them again.

I went back to work in June. Since then, I have fallen off ladders and jarred my back in ways that would cripple the normal man. But it seems that my back is made of iron. I am stronger than I have ever been in all my life.

Some of my friends were a little surprised that I went back to my old job as a construction man. They thought I would automatically become a preacher or a missionary. But I am still the same Fred Burdick. Oh, I love God with all my heart and I never pass up an opportunity to tell the men on my crew or my customers what God has done for me. No one is more grateful to God than I am.

I am still just a hard-working construction contractor. I spend most of my hours working around rough, tough men—brick layers, roofers, carpenters and plumbers. I am not a preacher and I don't try to act religious or pious. All I know is that once I was a hopeless cripple and now I am whole. And it was God who did it!

It used to bother me a little that folks thought I should have gone into the ministry or something. That is, it did until I ran across the story in the Bible of the man Jesus healed in the country of the Gadarenes. The man wanted to follow Jesus as an apostle, but Jesus said, "Go home to thy friends, and tell them how great things the Lord hath done for thee" (Mark 5:19). And that is what I have done.

At night, after a hard day's work, no one will ever know what it means when I sit down at a table and hear little Lisa as she bows her head and says, "Thank You, Lord, for healing our Daddy." She will never forget.

Neither will I.

3

Ours Not To Reason Why
by Clair B. King, M.D.

I have the highest regard for the medical profession—and from my conversations with doctors, it is my belief that one cannot be a doctor of medicine and not be religious.

It should not be amazing that we have doctors who tell of their personal experiences with their patients, as they witness divine healing through prayer. After all, all healing comes from God—a surgeon can perform surgery, but he must wait for a higher Power to do the healing; a doctor can prescribe medicine, but it takes God to heal.

Dr. King has practiced ophthalmology in Canton, Ohio, since 1935. Prior to that time, he was in general practice in Canton for ten years. A member of the American Academy of Ophthalmology and a past president of the Stark County Medical Society, he is on the staff of the 750 bed Aultman Hospital. He holds M.S. and M.D. degrees from the University of Pennsylvania, is a member of the Order of St. Luke the Physician, and an active leader in Christ United Presbyterian Church in Canton.

Miracles, by their very nature, defy scientific explanation. Defining a miracle is like defining infinity or eternity. It is impossible to know the mind of God, and therefore, impossible to fathom out His ways. Miracles can never be understood, they can only be accepted.

I believe in miracles, not only because I have seen them (and I have seen many), but because I believe in God. Even though I cannot understand or explain what takes place when a person is miraculously healed of some injury or disease, nevertheless, because I believe in God, I accept it. (I cannot understand radio and television either, but that does not prevent me from enjoying them.)

Divine healing is not a substitute for medicine or surgery, but is complementary to scientific medicine. Doctors are but instruments in the hands of God. And the fact that God sometimes chooses to heal without the help of His instruments should be a cause of rejoicing rather than confusion.

I have not always held these viewpoints, although I have been a Christian for many years. In fact, it was several years after my first experience with the power of God to heal that I realized what had happened.

It was in August, 1953, when five-year old Robert Kasner was brought to me for treatment of an injured eye. The cornea had been slashed by a piece of flying glass. The clear liquid in the front chamber of the eye had drained out, and the iris was protruding from the laceration.

My son, who is in practice with me, and I performed emergency surgery at Aultman Hospital. The iris was reset in its proper position and a conjunctival flap carried down like a patch over the wound.

Twelve days later, on a Saturday morning, we removed the dressing, only to find that the patch had not held. The iris was protruding through the cornea again. Surgery was again indicated, and an appointment was made for an operation on Tuesday, three days later.

We let the parents take the child home over the weekend, but Tuesday morning he was on the operating table being prepared for surgery. Before we administered the anesthetic, I made a final examination of the eye. I could not believe what I saw and called my son to examine him. The eye was completely healed. There was nothing on which we could operate. We were astonished, even a little embarrassed. I had no choice but to dismiss the surgical staff and have the lad wheeled back to his room.

I called the boy's parents and their reply was simple and to the point. "We took Robert to a Kathryn Kuhlman service on Sunday. Prayer was offered for his healing."

Six days later, I examined the eye again. "Well healed; good cosmetic appearance," I wrote on the boy's chart.

On January 9, 1954, nearly four months later, the report I jotted on the lad's file was, "Media clear; fundus negative." At that time, it was incomprehensible to me and I filed the case away to gather dust.

But then in 1957, after attending a service at Emmanuel Episcopal Church in Cleveland where Emily Gardiner Neal spoke on divine healing, I began to realize there was more to healing than performing surgery and administering drugs. I bought her book, _A Reporter Finds God Through Spiritual Healing_, and pored through it. I had always believed that religion healed the soul and medicine healed the body. Could it be possible that God also healed bodies?

I had been taught in medical school that it was medicine that healed and it was doctors who administered the medicine. People are materialistic, I thought, and therefore, they can only be treated with materialistic drugs and means.

Now I understood, for the first time, that people are both materialistic (flesh) and spiritual (spirit); and God, the Great Healer, often overrules His natural laws with supernatural laws of love and grace—and heals miraculously.

With this new understanding, I was in a receptive mood to listen to Dr. Alfred W. Price of Philadelphia when he lectured the next summer at Chautauqua, New York. We have a summer cottage there, but I had never paid any attention to the annual lectures on spiritual healing. Not only did I listen and comprehend, but I finished the week by joining the Order of St. Luke the Physician—an order devoted to the teaching and practice of spiritual healing.

Returning to Canton, I was determined to convince others that such healing is not only possible, but desirable. Some of my associates, especially my minister (who was a close friend), felt I was showing signs of a mental breakdown. However, since that time all ministers at Christ United Presbyterian Church have been inducted into the Order of St. Luke.

Shortly afterward, while spending some time in India as an interim medical missionary, I learned to pray aloud before an operation. All the missionaries did. When I returned to my practice, I felt if it was worth doing on the mission field, it was worth doing at home. Forestalling an injured professional pride, I determined

I would start praying aloud in the operating room before surgery. I have never regretted it.

It has changed the whole atmosphere of the operating room. Patients, nurses, assistants—all of us have been changed through the experience of going to God in prayer before the anesthetic is given. It is a thrill to be conscious of the fact that the Great Physician is by my side. His presence takes a large load of responsibility from my shoulders.

Not only did it make a difference in the operating room, but there was a decided difference in the patient's recovery. This was especially true among patients with emotional and spiritual problems who had received relief in those areas.

I still had doubts whether God would actually intervene because of prayer and invoke an instantaneous organic healing. I had always believed God could actually heal tissue instantaneously but never had conceded that He would. That is, until I remembered the Kasner case.

I went back and reexamined it. The corneal lesion had been perfectly healed, without even a scar. Only God could do this. And He did it in answer to Kathryn Kuhlman's prayer. I wanted to learn more about her, so I drove to Pittsburgh, Pennsylvania, to attend a miracle service. Later, I talked with her personally.

"I have nothing to do with these healings," she said. "It is all done by the Holy Spirit."

The fact that she was baffled by the healings convinced me that her ministry was genuine. She actually confessed to me that she never read books about divine healing because she wanted her mind to be a clear, pure channel to the power of the Holy Spirit.

"When I walk out on the platform," she said, "I depend utterly on God. I trust God for miracles to happen—and so they do. There is no mental block whatsoever."

This is the crux of spiritual healing. From a medical standpoint, there is no understanding—no explaining. We doctors have a little knowledge. Many times, this knowledge becomes a block to truth. Knowledge is not always the answer. We have to accept some things on faith.

This may be the reason Paul said, "But God has chosen the world's unschooled to shame the learned." (1 Corinthians 1:27, Berkley). And to reason out spiritual healing is just as impossible as it is to reason out God.

4

Canadian Sunrise

by Kenneth May

Mr. and Mrs. May live on a two hundred acre farm, producing grain and cattle in Forester's Falls, Ontario, Canada. His grandfather built their house in 1871 and Mr. May is the third generation to live there. They have two married daughters, one living in Lachine, Quebec, and the other in Pittsburgh, Pennsylvania. He was fifty-nine years old when this story began in the summer of 1966.

The sun had already dropped below the horizon and twilight was fading when I parked the tractor behind the barn and walked wearily across the backyard toward the old, two-story house that had been my home since birth. Our red and white collie fell in step behind me, reaching up to lick the salt that had collected on my hand during a long day's work in the fields. I was bone tired and the thought of Margaret's hot biscuits and a long, soaking bath made me want to hurry up and get inside.

I climbed the steps to the little porch on the back side of the kitchen, knocked the dirt from my shoes, and pulled the remaining straw off my wet shirt. "Did you get the hay finished?" Margaret called from the stove as she wiped her brow with her apron.

"Yes, but it's a good thing I only have to do it once a year. I don't think I could take it."

"Kenneth," she said with her laughing brogue, "remember you're not as young as you used to be. You will be sixty next birthday."

"Ummm, don't remind me," I said as I walked through the kitchen to wash up before supper. I glanced around at the old house. You're almost a hundred years old, old girl, I mused to myself. You've been doctored up, but after so many years, I guess a thing just naturally wears out. Maybe that's what is happening to me, too. Maybe I'm just wearing out.

I put my left hand under my right arm and gingerly felt the big lump that was developing in my armpit. I wonder if this is the beginning of the end, I thought.

I walked back through the house to the kitchen. Supper was almost ready and I stood gazing out the window at the last streaks of the magnificent sunset. Next door, silhouetted against the darkening sky, was the old cemetery. It separated us from the small church that stood alongside the road leading to Cobden. The ancient tombstones, weathered and battered from time and elements, seemed to beckon stealthily. Despite the warm weather, I felt a cold chill and shuddered involuntarily.

I had been close to death before. Back in 1945, I had been taken by ambulance to Pembroke Hospital in critical condition from pneumonia. I remembered hearing the doctors whisper to Margaret that I was on the verge of death. I prayed—desperately. I wasn't afraid to die, but I prayed God would let me live long enough to see my children raised. The next day, my fever had subsided and I was able to go home shortly with no bad after-effects.

Then, last year, our younger daughter had married and moved away from home. I was happy for her, but inside there was a dark foreboding that my borrowed time was now finished.

The last shreds of daylight disappeared and darkness enveloped the countryside. Only the lights in the little church beyond cast a reflection on the old tombstones that stood askew above the graves. I'm not afraid to die, I thought, for beyond the grave lives God. I slid my hand under my arm again and pressed the large knot in the armpit. But, I wondered, is this the way it's going to happen?

Margaret's cheery voice interrupted my gloomy thoughts and I walked into the kitchen to join her at supper.

That night, after my bath, I stretched out on top of the sheets with my hands behind my head. The light breeze coming through the bedroom window felt refreshing. Margaret had dressed for bed and was reaching for the switch on the lamp when I heard her exclaim, "What's this, Kenneth?"

I could sense the alarm in her voice and opened my eyes to see her staring at the big lump under my right arm, which was clearly visible. I glanced down at the protrusion. "Oh, that's been coming for some time now. I just never mentioned it."

"Why, it's the size of a goose egg. I think you ought to have Dr. Pye take a look at it. But I know you," she chided, "you will work until you drop dead out there in the barley and then I'll be left all alone."

There it was again; the thought of death. I quickly put it out of my mind and turned over on the bed, pulling the pillow under my head. "Well, let me finish with some of the chores and then I'll let him have a look at it. Probably it is just a swelling of some kind." But inside I had a gnawing feeling that it was more than that—far more.

Summer on a farm is not an idle time. We had twenty milk cows that demanded milking twice a day. With the exception of the pasture land, all the rest was under cultivation, which meant constant tending. The promise of a big harvest just weeks away was satisfying, but I was tiring easily and constantly plagued with sickening thoughts of the future.

A month later, Margaret finally talked me into going to see Dr. Mackercher. He suggested it might be a cyst and told me to wait another month and come back. But now it was August and we were beginning the harvest. As the weeks wore on, though, I noticed an extreme swelling in my right ankle. It became so bad I couldn't pull on my boots.

Evelyn, our younger daughter, was home from Ottawa for a weekend and between the two women, they finally wrangled my consent to make an appointment with Dr. Pye (whom Dr. Mackercher had suggested), one of the two doctors serving the little village of Cobden, nine miles away. I was scheduled to go in the following Tuesday. By this time, the swelling in my ankle had moved up my leg to my knee and the only way I could walk was stiff-legged.

Dr. Pye examined me and picked up the phone. "I am going to put you in the hospital and have that lump taken out," he said. "We can't tell much about this until we have a laboratory report."

The next day, Margaret drove me to Pembroke, fifteen miles the other side of Cobden along the Ottawa

River toward North Bay. Thursday morning, they took out the lump and sent it to the lab for a pathological report. They let me go home the following day and Dr. Pye said it would be a week before they got the pathologist's report. He asked Margaret to call him the next Saturday at the hospital.

I planned to do some light work around the farm the following week, but the swelling in my leg had moved up into the groin and lower abdomen. I began to bloat until I looked like a cow that had eaten too much alfalfa. The pressure in my stomach was almost unbearable and my leg hurt so much I couldn't stand on it. I spent most of the week lying on the sofa worrying about the harvesting which was being done by a hired man.

Margaret called Dr. Pye the next Saturday. He was evasive and said he would talk to us in person An appointment was made for us to come to his office Tuesday afternoon, Monday being Labor Day. Margaret nor I discussed it over the weekend, but I had a sinking feeling in the pit of my stomach that things must be pretty bad or he would have discussed it over the phone.

Monday night, while we were sitting at the table, the phone rang and Margaret got up from the table to answer it. It was Dr. Pye. "Tell Kenneth he's to be in Ottawa tomorrow at 1 P.M. to enter the hospital," he said.

"But," Margaret objected, "we're supposed to be at your office tomorrow."

"No," the doctor said, "I want you at the hospital in Ottawa instead. I'm at my office right now and I'd like to talk to you as soon as possible."

Margaret hung up and turned to me. "Why don't you finish your supper first," she said as she related the parts of the conversation I had not heard. But I had lost all my desire to eat.

I shook my head glumly and pushed my chair back. "We had better be going," I stated. "It will be dark before we get to town."

It was dusk as we drove along the country road into the small village that nestled against Muskrat Lake. The lights in the isolated farm houses blinked on as the last streaks of daylight disappeared from the sky.

Dr. Pye was waiting for us in his office. He motioned us to a chair and sat down behind his desk. "The news I have is not good," he said, his face ashen in the soft, overhead light. "The lab report showed the lump we removed was cancerous."

He paused to let the effect of his words soak in. "You have a condition known as Hodgkins Disease...cancer of the lymph glands."

He was trying to break it to us gently, but how can you soften a death sentence? Margaret's voice was trembling as she asked, "What does all this mean, Doctor?"

"It means," he said, getting up from his desk and coming around beside us, "that Kenneth will never live to be an old man." He pulled up a chair and sat down as though the weight of the world were on his shoulders. I could sense his deep feeling of concern, yet his frustration at not being able to do anything about it.

"How long do I have, Doctor?" I finally managed to ask.

He sighed, as if was were the one question he hoped I would not ask. "You have from months to five years left...certainly no more."

It was a difficult trip back home. Neither of us spoke as I drove slowly down the old, familiar road. Fifty-nine years is a long time to live in one house, know the same neighbors, travel the same road. As a boy, I had traveled this road from Cobden in a horse and wagon—only it was dirt then and not black asphalt. Growing up, I had driven my Dad's old car down this same road while I was courting Margaret. I had been so deeply in love, I never gave much thought to the future; I never dreamed I would one day travel it with only months to live.

We rounded the curve where the road branches off to Beachburg and then across the river to Ft. Coulonge. I remembered that romantic night so many years ago when Margaret and I were returning from the river. We had just set our wedding date and I misjudged the curve and almost went in the ditch. After that, I tried to keep both hands on the wheel while driving.

We drove on through the little settlement of Forester's Falls. My headlights reflected on the spire of the little United Church building. We made the sharp turn and headed out into the darkness toward the farm. How familiar were those miles; miles my father and mother had traveled carrying us to church as children, miles Margaret and I had traveled carrying Roberta and Evelyn to church—miles we had ridden in grief when our loved ones had passed away.

It was an old friend, that road from Cobden to the farm, and each mile spoke to us of precious memories. It had been a good, full life and if my borrowed time had run out, then I was ready to meet my Master.

I still had hope. Maybe all people feel this way when they have been told they have only a short time to live. I do not know, maybe it was just my will to live that was still alive. Whatever it was, I was determined I would not lie down and die peacefully. If God was calling me home, He would have to take me kicking and struggling all the way to the gates of Heaven.

We pulled into the driveway and Margaret started into the house. The supper dishes were still on the table where we had left them what seemed like an eternity ago. "Aren't you coming in?" she asked, getting to the bottom step and looking back.

"I'll be in shortly," I said, "you go ahead."

She turned and took a step back toward the car. "Are you all right, Kenneth?" she asked with concern.

"Yes, I am all right," I replied. "I want to check the stock and I'll be right in."

She turned and entered the house, the screen door shutting softly behind her. Our big collie came romping out of the stable and danced around in front of me. I ruffled his ears with one hand and started toward the barn. My right leg hurt so badly, I almost cried when I walked. Sitting in the car had stiffened it and I felt as if I were walking on a stove pipe—every step was jabbing sharp edges up into my groin and hip.

After checking the barn, I walked around the other side of the house and stood for a moment looking at the old cemetery beyond our property. In the distance, the ancient church building stood bleakly against the dark sky. Overhead, a billion stars twinkled in the crisp air as the last breeze of summer sighed through the trees. In the distance, I heard the faint sound of a barking dog. Everything else was still.

"Oh, God," I prayed, "once before you intervened in my life and healed me. This time my girls are gone and I have nothing to offer except myself. But if You will heal me, I will serve You in whatever way You ask. If it is Your will that I die, please let me die quickly and without pain."

My grandmother had died of cancer in this house and so had my father. The aura of death seemed to hang heavily in the atmosphere.

The stars became blurred as my eyes filled with tears. I glanced once more at the old graveyard, at the church beyond, and then at the glittering stars shining from their eternal sockets in the clear Canadian sky. I turned away and entered the house. On the morrow, I would drive the eighty miles to Ottawa to begin the treatments.

It was arranged for me to stay with Evelyn who was teaching school in Ottawa. Margaret could not stay since someone had to maintain the farm. The cows had to be milked, fodder had to be brought in, and the rest of the crops had to be harvested. Fortunately, I had finished the threshing and a neighbor had helped me with the combine the week before.

Every weekday morning for five weeks, a driver from the Cancer Clinic picked me up and took me to the General Hospital for the cobalt treatments. The technician would mark my body with an indelible pencil, much like a butcher marks a carcass before carving. Then the machine would be lowered to my flesh and while the technicians hid behind their protective lead shields, the cobalt rays were flashed into my body. When I returned to Evelyn's apartment, I would douse the upper part of my body with generous amounts of corn starch to keep down the skin burn from the radiation.

The second week, I came home for the weekend. It was late Friday evening when we arrived and I went straight to bed, worrying about the fields that needed to be plowed for the winter. Early the next morning, I dragged myself from the bed and hobbled to the window. I could not believe my eyes. Instead of corn stalks and ugly furrows, the fields were all freshly plowed. I turned and saw Margaret smiling through her tears. "Last Wednesday," she said, "the entire farming community turned out to do the plowing. There were thirteen tractors and they got it done in one day."

Only among people who love one another could this happen, I thought.

The cobalt treatments were relatively painless, but I could not see any progress in my condition. When I was finally allowed to come home, I still could not be up and around. I had to keep my leg elevated because of the pain.

The lumps gradually returned. All winter, I tried to convince myself that the cobalt had arrested the growth of the cancer cells, but each time I felt my body I knew it was only make-believe.

This time they began in the groin; just small lumps at first—kernels. But they were growing progressively larger. Then a large lump began to appear on my left chest, just below my collarbone.

Dr. Pye was examining me on a regular basis, but he said my system had absorbed all of the cobalt it could stand. "If you go back to the hospital, they will have to treat you with uranium or X-ray," he said.

By December of the following year, I had no choice. I had to return to the hospital in Ottawa. I had lost the use of my left arm because of the lump in my left chest. This time the treatment was X-ray.

I was allowed to return home after Christmas that year, but almost immediately I began to notice new swellings all over my body. I noticed the first ones when I was shaving. Tiny knots, like dried peas under the skin, had appeared overnight on my face just below my ear. Each morning when I shaved I could see they had grown larger until they were the size of small walnuts.

Others were developing in my neck and on my jaw. A large one appeared under my chin in the vicinity of my Adam's apple, giving me the appearance of having a double chin. My face was beginning to look disfigured and I knew I had only a short time to live as the lymph glands ceased to function properly.

In March of 1968, I returned to Dr. Pye. He phoned the specialist in Ottawa, trying to have me admitted to the hospital. He, too, sensed that the end was near. However, the hospital was full and the specialist indicated it would be a couple of weeks before they could take me. I went home, discouraged and afraid.

Margaret, who had been praying daily for my recovery, also discerned that time was fast running out. "I believe God is going to heal Kenneth," she told one of the neighbors. "He did it before."

"Yes, Margaret," the woman answered, "but remember that cancer is such a different thing than pneumonia."

Then came depressing news. Evelyn's husband had been transferred to Pittsburgh in the States. We had wanted them to be close as the days grew shorter. Roberta's family was till in Ottawa, but I was afraid we would not be able to see Evelyn again until it was too late. I told Dr. Pye I wanted to visit my daughter in Pittsburgh before entering the hospital. He agreed, sensing this could be my last chance, and suggested we postpone the hospital appointment until I got back.

When one of our farming neighbors learned we were planning the trip to Pittsburgh, she said, "Oh, I do hope you will have an opportunity to visit a Kathryn Kuhlman service while you are there."

"Who is she?" I asked.

In answer to my question, she gave us a copy of *I Believe in Miracles*. We were supposed to leave on Friday and I read the book diligently from Tuesday until then.

I was impressed, deeply impressed. Can it be, I wondered, that God can heal someone in the advanced stages of terminal cancer? Can it happen to me?

Early Friday morning, we drove to Ottawa, where some friends of Evelyn's met us and drove us on to Pittsburgh in their car. We arrived on Saturday and spent a delightful weekend with Evelyn and her family. Even though it was never mentioned, just below the surface was the constant knowledge that this would probably be the last time we would ever visit them.

Monday, the first of April, Evelyn took us all downtown to the First Presbyterian Church for the Monday night Bible study conducted by Miss Kuhlman. I was greatly impressed by the service and afterward talked to some of those who attended regularly. They urged me to remain over for the miracle service Friday morning. "God can heal you, you know," one man said.

I knew He could. I just didn't know whether He would or not.

"Why don't you stay over," Margaret encouraged. "Evelyn will be glad to have you and you can fly back home Sunday."

I finally agreed. Margaret returned, leaving me with our daughter and her family. As the week wore on, I became more and more anxious about the service on Friday. My leg was hurting so badly I couldn't stand for more than a few minutes at a time. The lumps on my face and in my joints had become painful. I knew this was my last chance.

I prayed. Only God knows how much and how desperately I prayed. Friday morning, Evelyn called me to breakfast, but I declined. "Aren't you going to eat?" she asked.

"No, I've been reading in my Bible where difficult cases of healing can sometimes be handled only through fasting and prayer (cf. Matthew 17:14-21). This morning, I am going to fast and pray to God to heal me."

Evelyn put her arm around my waist. "I'm sure He will, Daddy. If He loves you as much as I do, then how can He help but heal you?"

We arrived early, having been warned that the crowds on the steps at the old Carnegie Hall were always large. How am I going to tough it out on this leg, I wondered as we climbed the steps and took our place at the rear of the ever-growing circle of people who pressed around the doors. I don't think I can make it unless I sit down, I worried.

I was impressed with the friendliness of the complete strangers who gathered around the door. When they found out I was from Canada, several came over to talk. Then the oddest thing happened. A woman, a total stranger, came up and asked who I was. I told her and she said, "You have cancer, don't you?"

I was amazed, but thought she could probably tell from the lumps on my face or perhaps she had talked to someone who had been present Monday night. Before I could ask, she reached out, took hold of my arm and began to pray. I was embarrassed and felt awkward. But as she continued her prayer, I bowed my head and said from my heart, "I am Yours, Lord, do with me what you will."

I felt a strange sensation running through my body, a nervous tingling. The prayer was over and she said simply, "I know God will heal you." I started to thank her for her encouragement, but she melted into the crowd.

I turned to Evelyn, still embarrassed over what had just taken place, when I realized the pain had left my leg. It was gone. I remembered the specialist saying in Ottawa, "If we can ever cure the cancer, the pain in your leg will take care of itself.

I tried to speak, but all I could do was stutter. Evelyn's eyes were wet with tears. She did not know what was going on in my body, but she could see the joy in my eyes.

I stood the rest of the hour without feeling a trace of pain. When the doors opened, we moved with the crowd and were soon seated in the auditorium. We were surrounded by a warm noisiness—not loud, but the kind that gives you the feeling of belonging. The service started and I could feel the power and presence of God.

One of the staff workers came to me and said softly, "You are from Canada, aren't you?"

"Yes," I answered, assuming some of the people on the steps had told her."

"How do you feel?" she asked.

"The pain in my leg is gone," I said. "I think something has happened to me; I am sure something has happened!"

She ushered me to the platform where I was introduced to the crowd. Miss Kuhlman quizzed me about my condition and then told me to go home and have the healing verified by my doctor. She reached up and gently laid her hand on my shoulder as she began to pray. Suddenly I felt the warmth and overwhelming power of the Holy Spirit.

I am going to fall down in front of all these people, I thought. I resisted, trying to keep on my feet, but to no avail. I tried to get back up, but could not. While I was lying there, I heard a voice—as plain as day—saying, "You are healed, Kenneth May."

"That I am," I replied out loud. "I was healed outside the door." And I got to my feet and walked from the platform like a normal man. The limp was gone. The pain was gone. I could sense the swelling leaving my leg. I had been healed.

I walked back to the lobby and stood leaning against the wall while the water poured off me as if I had just spent an hour cutting hay in the hot sun. Then I began to shake. Crouching against the wall as I tried to control my body, I shook as if I would shake the building down. Eventually, it subsided and I returned to my seat beside Evelyn.

I spent most of the next day, Saturday, on the sofa in Evelyn's living room, shaking. The water literally poured out of the pores of my skin. Twice I had to get up and change clothes because they were wringing wet.

Sunday, they put me on a plane for Ottawa. My eyes were watering so badly that Evelyn was afraid I couldn't see, but I assured her that I was all right. I didn't know what was happening. But I was convinced it was associated with my healing. Margaret met me at the airport and we drove back to Forester's Falls.

Three weeks later, I kept my appointment at the Clinic prior to my admittance to the hospital. Margaret and I both knew that a dramatic change had taken place in my body, but we said nothing to the specialist. I knew he would find that the lumps had virtually dissolved and the swelling disappeared from my leg.

Following the examination, I returned to the waiting room. "I would like you to wait and have another doctor examine you," the first doctor said.

I agreed and we waited until all the other patients had gone and once again entered the examining room. The second doctor gave me a thorough checkup and then turned and looked at his colleague. "What am I supposed to find?" he asked, with a puzzled look on his face.

I interrupted him and asked, "What did you find, Doctor?"

He shook his head. "Nothing," he said and walked out.

The first doctor looked confused as he said, "If you will come back in another month, we will have our chief specialist examine you. However, I think you can forget about going into the hospital for awhile."

"What does that mean?" I asked.

"I cannot say anything until the other doctor examines you," he said. "Besides, it is too early to make a definite diagnosis of your present condition."

A month later, I returned for my last visit at the Cancer Clinic. The chief specialist examined me and when he finished, I said, "What do you find, Doctor?"

Like the other doctor, he gave me a strange look and said, "Nothing!" That's all he said.

I dressed and returned to the sitting room where Margaret was waiting. Moments later, the doctor appeared and walked straight over to her. He was a man of few—very few—words. He looked her straight in the face and said, "He is a very well man." He shook his head and repeated it as if he did not believe it himself, "...a very well man."

Margaret's face was beaming and her eyes were moist with tears. "It is a miracle, Doctor!"

He paused for a long moment and then said, "Yes, it is," and he shook his head and walked back through the swinging doors into the Cancer Clinic.

The summer sun was just setting over the tops of the tall spruce pines as we drove out of the big city into the rolling hills of our native Canada. The miles slipped by in silence as we both sat absorbed in our own thoughts. It has been a long time since I had noticed the brilliant beauty of a Canadian sunset.

As the sun sank out of sight and twilight settled across the pastoral countryside, I turned to Margaret and said, "God is good, isn't He?"

"Yes, He is everything," she answered quietly, still engrossed in her own thoughts. We drove on into the deepening darkness.

In front and overhead I could see the first glints of the evening stars and far to the north there were brilliant glimpses of the flickering aurora borealis. "I think I will get up early tomorrow and help with the milking," I said. "No sense in a well man sleeping late when there are chores to be done."

Margaret reached over and touched my arm with her hand. I could feel the warmth of her love in the silence of her smile. "Besides," I said, "I feel like watching a sunrise for a change."

"We will watch it together," Margaret said. "It will be good to welcome in a new day."

5

From Russia to Love
by Ritva Romanowsky

Ritva Romanowsky is a native of Finland. She came to the USA in 1953 with her husband, Arkady, a former officer in the Russian army, who now works as an auto mechanic in Southern California. She studied music at Helsinki Conservatory and is a devout Roman Catholic. They are parents of ten children and live in Tarzana, a suburb of Los Angeles.

It was spring in Finland in 1945 and the gay sounds of Helsinki and the smell of approaching summer were in the air. The long war was finally over. The girls in our Mission High School divided their time between witnessing of Christ on the street and normal girlish pranks.

But all was not so gay in other quarters. Hundreds of tired, anxious men were returning from the war, released from prison camps and discharged from the military. There was no employment and many were living desperate lives in the modern catacombs of the church basements.

After graduation, I found myself at my grand-aunt's seventy-fifth birthday party and was introduced to Arkady, a young Russian officer who had been captured, had turned his back on communism and was now assisting the Finns with their anti-communist propaganda broadcasts. He was one of those victims of war, mystically misplaced in a strange land.

We were living in the same neighborhood and began seeing each other on a regular basis. I was a believer while he was of the world, but we were still drawn to each other. That fall, before I entered Helsinki Conservatory to study voice and piano, we announced our engagement. Nine months later, we were married before a Lutheran and an Orthodox pastor, neither of whom would speak to each other aside from their official duties. Yet they both claimed to love the same Jesus.

Politically, times were getting difficult for little Finland. Stalin's agents were in every city and the communists were desperately seeking to gain control. Our neighbors were disappearing during the night as the communists would make night arrests. Arkady warned me that it could happen to us at any time.

Then it did happen. They came for Arkady late one night when I was preparing the bassinet for our soon to be born child. However, he dramatically escaped and we fled into the night on our long journey to freedom and eventually to America. But first there was a seven-month hideout with the underground, then an escape to Sweden and finally a tragic shipwreck in the English Channel that landed us in Ireland. It took six years before we finally reached the shores of freedom in America.

But merely having political freedom did not release us from the bondage of tyranny of sin and self. We had four boys by now and were living in a cramped New York apartment. Arkady heard of an opportunity to become an auto mechanic in Los Angeles, so we moved all the way across the country—still seeking that freedom for which we had dreamed so long.

I remembered my days in the Mission High School and that wonderful feeling I'd had when I knelt at the altar during an evangelistic meeting and accepted Christ as my personal Saviour. I remembered the good feeling I'd had attending the morning, noon and evening prayer meetings, as well as the Sunday services. Perhaps a return to organized religion would give me the release I needed, I thought.

While in Ireland, I'd been drawn to the Catholic services. I had attended both Finnish and Russian Orthodox churches in America, but was not satisfied. Failing to find satisfaction in any of the known institutions, I finally joined a Roman Catholic church in Los Angeles.

Then a tragedy hit. Arkady was in a car accident and one leg was placed in a cast for six months. He was left with a stiff knee, too crippled to continue his job. He gave up his work as an auto mechanic and bought a bar in Los Angeles. The bar soon failed financially, leaving us nothing but a bunch of beer drinking friends who helped make our home a squalid assortment of parties. I was miserable.

Then my ninth child was born. It was in 1961 and when I returned home from the hospital, I knew at once that something was wrong with me. I had received a spinal injection that somehow affected my entire nervous system. I was an emotional wreck.

The year before, when our eighth child was born, my spine had been accidentally damaged in a spinal anesthesia. I had gradually recovered, but the second spinal renewed the entire ordeal with all the accompanying symptoms—unbearable pain and headaches, dizziness, blackouts, loss of memory, and along with it, the depression. It was as if the lights had been turned out and the technicolor world had moved into black and white.

I had always been a strong, healthy woman. My Scandinavian background left little room for me to play the part of the sickly housewife who was run ragged by a houseful of little children. I loved my children and had always commenced each day with an energetic enthusiasm.

But now I was afraid to face the morning and cried throughout the day for no reason. The dark house haunted me with thoughts of death.

The gynecologist sent me to a specialist in internal medicine, who sent me to a neurosurgeon, who referred me to a psychiatrist. They loaded me down with pills, but nothing helped. At least the pills did not seem to do much good, although I was taking them by the handful.

Then I tried liquor. Although I had never drunk heavily, now I began to drink early in the morning as soon as Arkady left the house. By the time the older children got home from school, I was almost useless to help. And no one warned me that a combination of pills, which were both stimulants and depressants, and the liquor could be fatal. It was not long before I was in horrible shape.

Night after night, I lay on the couch and watched Arkady come in from work and put an apron around his waist to begin cooking dinner. The house stayed a wreck and the children needed attention since they received none from me during the day.

Five children under six can try the patience of any man. Yet he was the kindest, gentlest man I had ever seen. I often wonder if his disciplined patience was the result of those long years as a Russian army officer and subsequent years in a Finnish prison.

It was hopeless to help Arkady. All I could do was lie on the sofa and watch him with glazed eyes while he changed the baby's diaper and washed dishes. Our money for pills had run out and cheap wine was all the medication I could afford.

Good friends brought water from Lourdes for me to drink in hopes I could be healed of the spine condition, the arthritis which had set in or perhaps my diabetic condition. But nothing happened. I even visited a Catholic priest who had the gift of healing in his ministry, but it was not in God's timetable for me to be healed yet.

We sold the house and moved to the country and I thought for a while that I was improving, but the pain and depression returned with devastating regularity. How I wished to be dead! God seemed to hear my every prayer, but not this one. Somehow I knew that God wanted me to walk closer with Him, and then He would heal me.

We moved back to Los Angeles. I knew I had to find something to regain the joy of living. I could not go on like this. Even suicide seemed more attractive than the prospect of another tomorrow.

I thought if I could get out of the house, it would ignite a spark of interest in life. But even getting out was a chore. Los Angeles used to be such a beautiful city, but on that first day out, it seemed dark and dull—just like everything else in my life.

Browsing through a market, I absently picked up a book from the shelf, *Tell No Man*, by Adela Rogers St.

Johns. Maybe this would help, I thought. Something compelled me to dig into my purse for the price. We could not afford it, but at least it would help keep my mind off myself.

Once into its pages I could not put it aside. If only God can touch my life again, I thought. Finishing the book, I knew one thing: Jesus Christ was the only way for my life.

I renewed my vows to the Catholic church and tried to be faithful at Mass. But my physical condition grew steadily worse. The pain started at the bottom of my spine and ran up across my shoulders and into the back of my head. The only way I could move around the house was in a bent-over position.

The misery grew worse. And then I discovered I was pregnant again. "I don't think I can stand another baby," I cried. But it was not another—it was two. When the doctor told me I was carrying twins, I almost lost control. The old depression returned and I found myself facing a despairingly hopeless future.

The babies were born in September, 1967, after fourteen hours of hard labor, but one of them died at birth. I had begged the doctors not to give me another spinal, but since I was a charity patient the warnings were disregarded and a spinal anesthesia was administered. When I returned home from the hospital, the horrid spinal pain returned. The doctors told me to stay home and get plenty of rest. With ten children, they prescribed rest!

It wasn't a pretty picture. We were foreigners in a strange land. Neither of us could speak the language very well. Arkady was struggling to bring home enough money to keep a roof over our heads and buy food. My body was wracked with intense pain as I tried futilely to claw my way up from the black pit of depression. I even felt cut off from God. What could I do? Where could I go?

While lying on the couch one afternoon, the phone rang. It was a lovely Welsh lady, Mrs. Ivy Thompson, whom I had met a year earlier. She wanted to come over and see the babies. I remembered her as afflicted with multiple sclerosis, but when she entered the house, she was a different woman. She looked wonderfully well—twenty years younger.

"What has happened to you?" I exclaimed.

"I found Jesus and He healed me," she said simply as she smiled. "I now sing in the Kathryn Kuhlman choir at the Shrine. Why don't you come to the next meeting with me?"

I was touched by her concern, but far less than enthusiastic over the idea of attending a healing service. "You know I am Catholic," I said. "I'll never let a non-Catholic lay hands on me."

But I pondered the invitation for almost two months. Then one rainy Sunday morning in November, I got up and attended early Mass. I had just returned home when Mrs. Thompson called. "Miss Kuhlman is at the Shrine Auditorium today. We will be leaving here at 11:30 A.M. Why not come with us?"

"No, Ivy," I said. "I just don't care to go. I can't bring myself to believe in this kind of thing. Besides, it is raining."

"Nonsense," she said, "come on over here. I've been preparing you for this time." I found later she meant she had been praying for me.

I finally agreed, just to be polite. My back was hurting dreadfully and I was glad I had an appointment with the doctor the next morning. But I got in my car and drove around to the Thompson's house. They were waiting for me when I pulled up in the driveway.

I painfully climbed into the back seat and we started our drive across the city to the Shrine. As we sped along the Hollywood Freeway, the tires of the car singing against the wet pavement, Mrs. Thompson began to sing softly, too. I listened to her words, "Spirit of the living God...."

I started to hum along when suddenly I had a strange sensation in my back. It was a mysterious, tingling sensation that started in my head and ran down my spine. I actually heard a crackling noise in my backbone.

I was scared and confused and looked up to see if either of the Thompsons had noticed anything. Obviously not, for Mrs. Thompson continued to sing as the rain peppered the windshield.

I gingerly sat back in the seat and closed my eyes. Something had definitely touched my body—something supernatural. The pain had left. It had vanished completely. On the outside everything seemed the same, but inside I felt as if I were a different person. I had no way of knowing, but this was the beginning of a series of events so remarkable that even I would have difficulty believing them.

We pulled off the freeway and drove the two blocks to the huge Shrine Auditorium. Mr. Thompson let us out and went on to park the car. Mrs. Thompson went through the side door to the choir and I told her I would meet them in front of the auditorium when the service was over.

Since it was still raining, the front doors had been opened early and I went in. I couldn't get over the vastness and beauty of the great auditorium. People were streaming in by the hundreds, trying to get the choice seats. I stood in the great lobby, looking around at the intense faces of those who were coming in out of the rain and hurrying through the little tunnels that led to the main auditorium.

I followed them into an entrance tunnel which led inside. I only took a step or two into the awesome auditorium when I felt a strange sensation come over me. My legs began to buckle. I wasn't fainting, because I had complete control of my mind, but I simply could not stand. Before I could grab hold of anything, I was on my knees in the aisle. "Heavens!" I said out loud. "What's wrong with me?"

People were streaming past, heading for the few seats that were still available in the front of the auditorium. I guess they thought I was praying, but I just could not stand up.

I grasped the arm of a seat and pulled myself to my feet, still shaking and unsteady. An usher approached and I asked him if I could sit down in one of the seats in a roped-off section. "I don't know what has happened to me," I told him. "My legs just gave out and I fell forward."

I found a seat and rested until the service began, trying desperately to understand what was transpiring in my life and body. First that strange feeling in the car—now this.

Kathryn Kuhlman called six young Marines to the stage for recognition. Many of us in the balcony stood, watching as she prayed for them. They all fell to the floor and I wondered what kind of hypnotism this was.

Suddenly and without warning, my own legs buckled again and I collapsed backward into my seat. I tried to get back to my feet, but the muscles in my legs refused to respond. What is this, I kept asking myself, my mind in a turmoil as I tried to figure out what was happening.

The service continued and she moved into her sermon. This is blasphemy, I thought. How can this woman claim that God is speaking through her? She is no priest. She is not even a nun.

At the close of her sermon, when she asked us to bow our heads, I did. "The Holy Spirit is here and He will give you your heart's desire if it is asked in Jesus' name," she said. "Just make your petition."

The least I can do is cooperate, I thought. I put my hands to my face and then it happened. Suddenly I was aware of the literal presence of Jesus Christ standing before me. It was so strong, I wanted to raise my head or peek through my fingers. I knew He was standing right there in front of me.

The thoughts raced through my mind like the cars whizzing by on the freeway. What should I pray for? What does He want me to say? What is the greatest need in my life? I opened my mouth and the words came tumbling out unexpectedly, "Forgive me my sins!"

I had no sooner uttered these words than I felt I was being literally immersed in the love of God. It was as though He were bathing me and baptizing me in His love.

The tears came then. I was not really crying, just overflowing with tears. I still had my hands over my face and the tears were streaming through my fingers. I knew I had to get to the front of the auditorium to tell Miss Kuhlman something wonderful had happened to me.

Again I was blocked by an usher. "Have you been healed?" he asked.

I was so caught up by the spiritual experience that I completely forgot about the experience in the car. "I don't think so," I replied. "I just want to tell Miss Kuhlman about this wonderful feeling in my heart."

No doubt the usher thought I was a crank. He kindly suggested that I take my seat and wait until the service was over. But I could not stay seated and tried twice more to get to the front. Each time, my way was blocked.

At last Miss Kuhlman gave an altar call and the aisles were filled with people streaming toward the stage. This is my chance, I thought, and I joined the procession heading for the platform.

We were ushered to a side room and after the service Miss Kuhlman herself came through the door where we were all waiting. Now is my time to tell her, I thought again. But instead I found myself shrinking back toward the far door.

Then came the time when Miss Kuhlman said, "There is a miracle far greater than the healing of the physical body; it is the spiritual healing for the soul. Jesus said, 'Ye must be born again.' The one thing we all have in common is the first birth (the birth in the flesh), but to be born of the Spirit, you must accept what Jesus Christ did for you on the cross."

I was suddenly afraid. I didn't understand and I opened the back door and made my way out to the street. I should have stayed, I thought, but my footsteps carried me farther and farther away from the place where she was.

The Thompsons picked me up in front of the auditorium and we began the long drive back across the city. They wanted to know all about my sensations and I told them of my final fears in letting Miss Kuhlman pray for me. When we got home, Mrs. Thompson insisted I come in for awhile. Once inside the house, she turned to me and said, "Ritva, let me pray for you."

I looked up and saw her coming toward me, her hands extended to put them on my head. "No!" I screamed as I jumped to my feet. "No!" And I literally ran from the house, down the steps to my car, and hurriedly backed into the street. A great wave of remorse swept over me. That was a poor way to treat a friend, I reproved myself, especially after that wonderful experience at the Shrine. But I headed down the street toward home.

My mind flashed back to the cleansing, baptizing sensations that had been mine in the balcony at the Shrine. Suddenly I felt a wonderful song of praise and adoration bubbling up in my heart. I began to sing. Even though I often sang in my native Finnish tongue, this time the words and music were totally unfamiliar. It was a strange, unknown tongue. I had no idea what I was singing, but I knew it was a song of praise and I didn't want to stop. I continued down the street, singing from the bottom of my heart—but letting the Holy Spirit supply both the music and the lyrics.

I stopped at the market to pick up some bread and milk for the children and I was scarcely able to control the indescribable happiness I was feeling. Once back in the car, I was again singing in the strange, unknown tongue. It was so wonderful!

As I pulled up and stopped in front of the house, I wondered what I would tell Arkady and the children. I didn't even know what had happened. How could I tell them? I decided I would say nothing. If this was real, they would soon find it out. If it was not real, then I wouldn't have made a fool of myself in front of them.

I did not have to wait long to find out. The children could tell the difference the moment I walked into the house. "Mama, something has happened to you. Your eyes—they sparkle!"

I bent down and pulled them to me. How wonderful it was to be able to bend over and not be in pain. How wonderful it was to feel the happiness that surged from their hearts to mine! How wonderful it was to be alive.

It was not many days before Arkady said in his quiet way, "Something has changed about you, Ritva."

"You notice?" I said.

"I cannot help but notice. You are healthy. But even more important, you are happy. What has happened?"

That was all I had been waiting for, and that evening I poured out my heart to my kind and gentle husband. "There has been a change," I said. "I have been healed. Not only is the pain in my back gone, but the arthritis has disappeared. And the last medical check showed all the diabetes has vanished, too. And, Arkady, there's no more depression. Do you realize that I have not cried a single time since that Sunday?" He nodded, although his own eyes were moist at the time.

"And besides, Arkady, I have stopped taking medicine. I have not had anything, not even an aspirin, since that day. And no more liquor either."

"I know," he said softly, smiling, "I know."

Arkady's background was far different from mine. He was born in Warsaw, Poland, but at an early age moved to Minsk in White Russia. When he was thirteen, his parents were thrown into a political concentration camp from which they never returned. He and his young brothers and sisters were forced to beg in the

streets for scraps of bread until he found a job that en-
abled him to finish high school.

Having been raised under the communist government, he had always despised the church and organized
religion. His father had been an outspoken atheist who
had engaged in public debates with Russian priests during the Czarist regime. After leaving Ireland, he had been
sympathetic to the Catholic church, but had never made
any outward signs about joining. Therefore, I was afraid
he might be hostile toward my new found faith in God.
However, when he noticed the change that had taken
place in my body and life, he became interested, too.

Something else had happened to me. For the first time
in my life, I had a burning desire to read my Bible. I could
not get enough of it. After I got the children to bed, I read
far into the night. And many times I woke at 2 or 3 A.M.
and got up and read and prayed some more. I had
boundless energy and strength. It was an amazing transformation.

Mrs. Thompson asked me to write Miss Kuhlman and
tell her what had happened to me. I objected, saying, "She
must get mail from a million people. She would not be
interested in me." But Mrs. Thompson was remarkably
insistent and a month later, I wrote Miss Kuhlman a note.

So much had happened, but all of our problems had
not been settled. Our eighteen-year old son, Peter, was
still living 450 miles north in San Rafael, rebelling against
home and society. It had been five months since we had
heard from him, although I learned from some friends
that he had been smoking marijuana. Many hours were
spent in prayer for him.

Two months after my experience at the Shrine, my
prayer time was interrupted by the ringing phone. It was
Peter. For some mysterious reason he had decided to
come home for a weekend visit.

I redoubled my prayer efforts and asked Arkady if he would go with me to the Shrine service that coming Sunday. "If we take Michael (our next oldest son), perhaps Peter will consent to go also." Arkady agreed, not only to get Peter to attend, but because he wanted to go. We both knew it would take a miracle to change Peter's life.

But the miracle happened before Peter got home. He was hitchhiking outside San Francisco when a businessman from New Jersey stopped and picked him up. Once Peter was in the car, the man told him he had never picked up a hitchhiker before, much less one dressed like a hippie. The man was a Christian and began to witness to Peter about the Lord. As they sped along the coastal highway between San Francisco and Los Angeles, the Holy Spirit used the man's personal testimony and by the time they reached the outskirts of the city, Peter had accepted Jesus Christ as his Saviour. When the businessman let him out, he gave Peter his Bible, telling him to keep it and read it. Peter arrived home a changed person.

And so the four of us sat in the balcony that January Sunday in 1967. My heart was overflowing with praise to God, but when the service started, Miss Kuhlman said something that shocked me upright in my seat.

"I want to share a letter I received from a woman living in Southern California," she said as she began to read:

Dear Kathryn Kuhlman,

I am much late in writing to you that I was miraculously healed at the November meeting in the Shrine Auditorium in Los Angeles. A mother of ten living children, I am a Catholic, thirty-nine years old, and have been ill for the past six and a half years....

I could scarcely believe my ears. It was my letter. When she finished reading, she said, "I have no idea whether the writer of this letter is here or not. If she is here, I want her to come forward."

I do not know how it happened, but suddenly I was standing beside the woman that just two months before I had called a blasphemer. I blurted out, "My husband is up there in the balcony, too. He is from Russia. He served in the Red Army. Do you think Jesus can help him, too?"

"Certainly," she answered. "You call him."

"Arkady," I called into the microphone, scanning the vast sea of indistinguishable faces in the high balconies. "Come, come."

Moments later he was standing beside me professing his faith in the Christ who had changed my life and healed my body. "I have two sons up there, also, Peter and Michael. Can they come to Jesus, too?" I asked.

"Why, of course," Miss Kuhlman answered.

"Peter, Michael, come...you come," I called out. There was not a dry eye in the auditorium as my two sons joined us on the platform. It was a glorious day for us all.

Since that healing experience in the back seat of Mrs. Thompson's car, I have never taken another pill, and the liquor is still a thing of the past. Our family life is happier than it has ever been. The children are growing spiritually as we read our Bible in the home and pray.

God is so good. Now I know it makes no difference whether you are Finnish, Russian, or American—God knows no such thing as nationality.

6

The Man with Two Canes
by Harold Selby

That thou shouldst so delight in me
And be the God Thou art,
Is darkness to my intellect
But sunshine to my heart.

Mr. Selby is a graduate of the University of North-
ern Iowa, with majors in elementary education and
mathematics. He and his wife Arlene were living in
the small town of Conrad, Iowa, with their two adopt-
ed children when this story took place. Harold was
teaching fifth grade and Arlene was teaching remedi-
al reading in the high school. They now live in Elyr-
ia, Ohio.

There it was again! That strange twitching in my left
eye. I was standing on the school playground and
turned to one of the other grammar school teachers and
asked her if she noticed it. She did not seem concerned,
but deep inside I had an empty, scared feeling—like
something was wrong, very wrong.

There had been other strange symptoms during the preceding months like the temporary paralysis of my throat and extreme coughing spells. The doctor had given me pills to loosen my lungs and told me not to worry. But I still had a weird feeling that something drastic was about to happen.

Then on Saturday morning, January 15, 1966, I woke up so dizzy I could not see. My wife Arlene cancelled her Saturday morning piano students and took me to the doctor. He gave me a shot, but as I started out of his office, I collapsed. I did not faint, but I felt a tremendous pressure bearing down on me. My whole muscular system gave way.

Conrad is just a tiny little town and the doctor thought I should be hospitalized for tests. So Arlene drove me over to Marshalltown where I entered the hospital. They gave me all the basic tests: spinal tap, EKG, blood tests, the works. I felt better and the next Friday the doctor came in and said I could go home Sunday.

That night, I climbed out of bed at eleven o'clock to go to the bathroom and the pressure hit again. It knocked me to the floor and I had to be helped back to bed. When I regained my senses, I was seeing double.

Then came Sunday morning, the day I was supposed to go home. My doctor came in and checked my eyes and the next thing I knew, I was in an ambulance on the way to the hospital in Waterloo. I didn't know it at the time, but the doctor in Marshalltown had told Arlene he thought I had a brain tumor.

I spent the next nine days in the hospital in Waterloo where they ran more tests. "I think you've had a light stroke, Mr. Selby," the doctor said. "We're going to let you go home and we want you to keep in close touch with us." I felt relieved. I had no idea that while he was telling me this, he was writing on my chart the dreaded words: multiple sclerosis.

On February 14, I got my doctor's permission to resume my teaching duties on a part-time basis. Things went all right because I rested in the afternoon and the next Monday I decided to try it full-time. Wednesday morning, Arlene begged me to stay home, but I insisted that I was all right and went on to work. I drove the nine miles out to the elementary school, but by 10 A.M. I was so sick the secretary's husband had to carry me out of my classroom to the car.

"You can take me home. I'll be okay," I kept saying. But instead he drove me to the doctor's office. The doctor came running out to the parked car and examined me. Within minutes I was in an ambulance and on my way back to Waterloo.

This time I was in Waterloo Hospital only three days. After a quick examination, the doctors made arrangements for me to be admitted to Mayo Clinic in Rochester, Minnesota, as an outpatient.

By the time I arrived at Mayo, the pain was so severe that I had a numbness on the left side of my body from head to toe. I was seeing double and had little control of my bladder. I staggered when I walked and was shaking badly. When I tried to sit or stand, my head flopped from one side to the other as if there were no muscles in my neck. I was scared—scared to death of what the doctors were going to find.

I was in Mayo five days taking the full battery of tests: an electroencephalogram, blood tests, spinal tap (my fourth), and X-rays.

On the fourth of March, my wife's father and mother drove up from Conrad and took me home. The doctors at Mayo said they would send the doctors in Conrad and Waterloo the results of their examinations. I went home and waited.

About three weeks later, I went back to my doctor. He told me Mayo's diagnosis had confirmed the diagnosis at Waterloo. "You mean I've had a stroke?" I asked.

"I wish it were a stroke, Harold. But it looks like it's multiple sclerosis."

Multiple sclerosis, I thought. I knew absolutely nothing about the disease except what little I had read in the papers or learned when neighbors had come to the door to solicit for funds for national research. Now I found that my case was classified as incurable. There was no known way to alter or even slow the progression of the disease.

I couldn't believe this could happen just when everything seemed to be going so right. At thirty-three, I had felt I was well on my way to achieving my cherished goals in life. Arlene and I were both teaching. We had adopted two precious children. I was making plans to attend graduate school to complete my Master's Degree...and now, this.

Even though I was able to force myself to resume teaching, by the end of the school year I had become totally dependent on two canes which I had fashioned from discarded broomsticks.

I could not even walk up the steps to my office without stumbling. Even taking care of my own personal needs became a gargantuan task. I was taking eighteen pills a day: codeine, Darvon, pills for my lungs, etc.

I felt lost—more lost than I knew it was possible to feel. My life had always been full of action, devoted to meeting the needs of other people. I had taught and coached elementary school baseball and football. I even used to quarterback some of the student teams, but now my days of normal life were over. I could not walk, much less run.

Reading was virtually impossible. I could only drive short distances. Watching TV was a thing of the past. Even getting in and out of the bathtub became a major accomplishment. Everything I loved to do had been snatched away in just a matter of months.

I found myself asking God, "Why?" We had been active attenders at the Methodist church and my wife even played the organ. When the new minister had come to town, the old minister had said, "You will have at least one listener—Harold Selby." I had sung in the choir and taught Sunday school. But none of it had prepared me to face the loss of health and the hard, cold reality of death. And certainly there had been no mention of the healing power of the Holy Spirit. All I knew was that my life was over. I was doomed to spend the rest of my days as a semi-vegetable.

I tried everything. I consulted the Veteran's Administration in Des Moines to discuss the possibility of a rehabilitation program. The doctors at the hospital were dubious. They did not think I could qualify for VA help, but promised to look into it.

"Go home and let your wife take care of you," they had said. But what man wants to be dependent on his wife? Besides, Arlene had a full-time teaching job herself. How could she hold down a job and take care of me twenty-four hours a day? And now we were faced with another problem. We had used up all our savings and needed her income just to survive.

I was to find that the darkest hours always precede the dawn. And so, in an unsuspected and mysterious way, I was introduced to the power of God. And things began to happen so fast, they are hard even to relate.

It began in June. I did not want to let my legs get so stiff that I could not use them, so I was constantly walking. Late one afternoon, I decided to walk four blocks to the convalescent home to see a friend who also had multiple sclerosis. On the way back, I took a different street and passed in front of the Presbyterian pastor's house. Donald Shaw, the pastor, noticed me struggling down the sidewalk on my two canes. Even though we hardly knew each other, he called out and I stopped to chat for a moment.

"I have a book on healing that you might be interested in," he said as I was about to leave. To be polite, I took the book home and Arlene read it to me. It was *I Believe in Miracles*.

When I saw Donald Shaw a week later, he said, "Do you really believe God can heal people?" I sensed that he was a little unsure of himself, but it started me thinking. I knew some of the Bible stories about miracles in Jesus' time. But the thought of spiritual healing had never entered my mind—at least until that moment.

I thought for a minute and then answered, "Well, yes, I guess He can. He can do anything, can't He?"

Donald rubbed the back of his neck and gazed out across the backyard toward some huge Chinese Elms. "Yes, I know God *can* do anything. My question is whether He *will* or not."

The accounts of the miraculous healings in *I Believe in Miracles*, especially among people who had little faith, had ignited a spark of hope in my discouraged heart. Maybe, just maybe, God would heal me, too, I dared to think.

Donald Shaw moved to Kansas City a week later, just as he had said he was going to do. But I determined that I was going to learn as much about the power of God as I could. And it was this quest that led us to attend the Cedar Falls Bible Conference in Waterloo the last of July.

I had become accustomed to the spectacle I made when I staggered into a public meeting on my canes. My legs always acted as if they were about to collapse and my head jerked crazily in different directions. But nothing was going to stand in my way to find out about God's power.

As Arlene and I left the meeting the first day, we heard a familiar voice. The figure approached, but because of my blurred vision, I could not recognize him. "Harold, it is Don Shaw. Remember?"

Remember? He was the reason we were there. A wave of exhilaration swept over me. Was God really at work? Had He planned this? It was too mysterious for me to comprehend at that moment. Looking back, though, I can see the gentle, guiding hand of the Holy Spirit putting together the pieces of the puzzle—making a beautiful picture to glorify the Heavenly Father.

We spent the evening together talking about the power of God to heal the sick and wondering whether the miracle services were still being held in Pittsburgh. "Why not write Kathryn Kuhlman and find out?" Arlene suggested. The solution was so simple, we all marveled that we had not thought of it sooner.

The next day, we mailed two letters. One was simply addressed to Kathryn Kuhlman, Pittsburgh, Pennsylvania. The other was to the Pittsburgh Chamber of Commerce requesting information on the Kuhlman meetings. I had so little hope that the letters would ever reach their destinations, I went ahead with my plans for possible rehabilitation with the VA hospital.

Then Kathryn Kuhlman's letter arrived. Yes, they were still having services in Carnegie Hall. Yes, God was still healing people and she felt that He would heal me.

With this new hope, we made plans to attend the miracle service the following week. But we had used up all our money and there would not be any more until after school started and Arlene drew her first check. Pittsburgh was eight hundred miles away and we needed at least forty dollars to make the trip. So the week before we were to leave, I started out to earn expenses.

In eighteen hours, I had sold thirteen sets of the World Book Encyclopedia. I do not know whether the people felt sorry for me or whether I was just that good a salesman, but God was at work and we raised the money. On Wednesday, August 10, we headed out!

I was able to drive to Des Moines, where I took my final tests at the VA hospital. But after the battery of tests, my reflexes were so poor and my vision so blurred and fuzzy, I realized it was impossible for me to see well enough to drive any farther.

Arlene had always been terrified of driving in city traffic. When I told her I could not see, she began to cry. We sat there in the parking lot, completely frustrated. For the first time in my life, I asked God to help me. Oh, I had often prayed general prayers, but never any specific prayers. But this time I did. "Lord, be my eyes, be my strength."

Then, with new assurance, I said to Arlene, "Honey, God is going to guide us. If you will tell me where to turn, when to slow down, and when to speed up, then with the three of us, I know we can make it."

We pulled out into the heavy traffic with Arlene quietly saying, "Move to the left...slow down a little...steer to the right...get ready to stop...." And do you know what? God gave us the strength and ability to drive all the way to Pittsburgh without a single mishap. Arlene drove on the open road and I drove in the cities.

That first night, we stopped at a roadside park in Illinois to sleep in the back of the car. Something was already happening in my body. Never had I been so aware of the presence of God. For the first time in months, I was able to stagger around without my canes. I could hardly believe it. I leaned against the fender and cried. Arlene stood with her arms around my waist and cried with me. Something special was happening. We could feel it.

The second night, we pulled into Pittsburgh right at the evening rush hour. The lights of the cars were driving me crazy. I was trying to steer and Arlene was telling me where to go. How we kept from being killed or from killing someone else is simply another of God's miracles. But we managed to drive right to the parking lot at Carnegie Hall.

We planned to spend the night in the car again to conserve our dwindling supply of money. But a clerk at a nearby store advised against it. "Not here on the North Side," he said, "somebody will club you for sure!" He gave us directions to a hotel across the river. But when we crossed the bridge, our system of my steering and Arlene's navigating got crossed up. We took a wrong turn and never could find the highway again. We wound up spending the night in a cheap truck stop.

The next morning, we climbed the stairs of Carnegie Hall at eight o'clock. The services did not start for another three and a half hours, but there were people already waiting. "Surely God will honor you today," someone said when they found out who we were. They sounded so confident, so trusting, that our hopes soared.

The next three hours passed like seconds as we listened to the thrilling experiences of those around us who had been healed. And when the doors opened, I felt a new strength in my body that carried me through the crush of the crowd to waiting seats. There was an almost electric sensation of the Spirit of God moving through the great throng of people. I could feel it and I was too excited even to pray.

The music from the organ and piano carried me closer to God than I had ever been. Then suddenly Kathryn Kuhlman appeared on stage. The audience rose to their feet applauding. I finally got positioned and pulled myself up, too.

All around me, people were singing. Some were holding their hands in the air. I, too, wanted to raise my hands and join in, but I could not let go of the seat in front of me. "God!" I choked out. I could almost feel Him enveloping me with His love. It was marvelous.

Then the healings began. For an hour I sat in awe, listening to the testimonies of instantaneous healings. Then Miss Kuhlman asked the audience to stand and sing again. I staggered to my feet.

"Do not see Kathryn Kuhlman," she said from the stage. "Forget the one standing next to you. Look up and see Jesus, for He is the One who will give you the desire of your heart."

I leaned my canes against the back of the seat in front of me and took Arlene's hand. I glanced to the other side and noticed a wisened, little Negro woman with hands gnarled from many years of heavy toil. She was reaching out for my other hand. I hesitated only a split second, but my prejudices came bubbling to the surface and instead of extending my hand, I simply stuck out the last two fingers for her grasp. I felt her calloused hand close around them.

A great wave of conviction swept over me. "Lord, forgive me! I should have given her my hand."

Then it hit, like a tidal wave—like a great whoosh! It swept through my body from head to foot. It was a sensation much like a charge of electricity passing through my total being. It started on one side of my brain and came surging down through my body. I gasped for breath and my lungs were clear. I opened my eyes and I could see clearly. I felt my legs, back, and neck gaining strength. It was as though my whole body were being pricked by pins and needles.

Vaguely, I heard Miss Kuhlman say, "Someone out there has just been healed." I turned and looked at Arlene, but before she could say anything, I sensed it was me. When I saw one of Miss Kuhlman's staff members making her way between the seats, I left my two canes leaning against the back of the seat and made my way past four or five people out into the aisle.

I started to take her arm for support and then I thought, I do not need to hold on, I am healed. And I was. I walked unassisted down the aisle and up the steps to the platform. "When God heals you, you are healed," Miss Kuhlman said. "Run back down those stairs and put it to the test!"

I turned and bounded back down the steps like a school kid. I did not care what kind of spectacle I was making. When I returned to the stage, Miss Kuhlman asked if there were any present who could verify my story. Arlene came to the platform, her face wet with tears.

We stood for a long time, trembling in each other's arms. It was a moment I will never forget.

The miracles had just begun. It took a miracle to get us to Pittsburgh, but our money was almost gone and it was going to take another to get us home.

As we were leaving the auditorium, a complete stranger, Mrs. J. Ross Philips, came up and asked where we were spending the night. Arlene and I looked at each other and then confessed that we were sleeping in the back of our car. She insisted we follow her back to Poland, Ohio, and spend the weekend with her family.

We were hesitant about taking advantage of her generosity, so we spent Friday night in the back of our car. But the next afternoon we gave in and pulled up in front of the beautiful Philips residence in time for dinner and a sound night's sleep.

The next morning, we attended Miss Kuhlman's worship services in Stambaugh Auditorium in Youngstown. When the time came for the offering, I glanced quickly into my billfold. All I had was a ten-dollar bill. It was every cent that we had left. I whispered to Arlene, "I am going to put it in."

"Don't you dare," she shot back. "We've got to get back to Iowa."

"As much as the Lord has done for me, I just have to put it in. We will fast on the way back," I said. Arlene glared at me. She could not understand my sudden burst of generosity.

When Miss Kuhlman asked us to hold the money in our hands and pray before the offering was received, something happened to Arlene, too. After the prayer, she reached over and squeezed my arm. "Go ahead, honey, we will make it some way."

That afternoon Mrs. Philips fixed us a huge picnic supper and her husband loaned us his big thermos. We left about 5 P.M. "Why not take the turnpike?" they asked as we climbed into our car. "It will be much quicker."

But turnpikes cost money in toll fares, and I did not have the heart to tell our new friends that we did not have a single penny in our pockets. "No, we will go routes 224 and 24," I replied. "That way we can view the countryside."

As we drove into the twilight, Arlene gave a short gasp. "What's wrong, honey?" I asked.

"You forgot about the bridge across the Mississippi," she said. "There's a fifteen-cent toll."

"I guess we will have to stop and see your brother on the way back then," I said. "But I am not going to borrow more than fifteen cents."

We spent the night in the car outside Kentland, Indiana, and at 8 A.M. we pulled into a service station. "The car needs gas and I need a shave," I said. I had a credit card and wasn't worried about payment for the gas.

I felt refreshed after shaving and was ready to face the problems of the day with new vigor. Then a new barrier arose. "Sorry, Mister," the station attendant said as I handed him my credit card. "I can't accept this."

"What do you mean?" I stammered. "It says right here that your station honors these cards."

"Nope!" he replied, his Midwestern stubbornness much in evidence. "I've been stuck too many times."

"Well, you will take my check then, won't you? The gas was only $3.87."

"Nope! Won't take that, either."

I borrowed his phone and looked up the number of a local minister. I told him who I was and asked him if he'd cash my check for $3.87. He asked me where I was going and where I had been. I told him and added that I had been healed of multiple sclerosis.

"You've been what?" he asked, his tone of voice changing slightly.

"I've been healed," I bubbled over. "God healed me in a miracle service." And the line suddenly went dead. I turned to Arlene with a puzzled look and said, "He hung up." This was my first indication that everyone was not going to be as enthused over my healing as I was.

Arlene began to laugh. "Let's see how the Lord is going to get you out of this one," she giggled.

We tried the bank and another service station. Neither would help us. Finally, someone suggested that we call the local undertaker. He agreed to vouch for my check and lend us the fare for the toll bridge and we were on our way.

I recalled Jesus' words to the leper He had healed. "See thou tell no man..." (Matthew 8:4). I think I was beginning to understand why. But I also knew that nothing could keep me from testifying.

The first test came two weeks later when I resumed my teaching position. I had also been assigned the principal's job in addition to my teaching duties and I was determined that nothing would stand in the way of my witnessing. The children could hardly believe I was the same teacher they had seen struggling to school on two canes. When they asked me what happened, I told them about the miracle of my healing and of my commitment to Jesus Christ.

The real test came in March of the following year. My school superintendent came to me with a new contract. "We are pleased with your work, Harold," he said. "And we are prepared to give you an eight hundred dollar raise for the coming year." He paused, "But there is one stipulation. We would like you to promise us that you will stop talking to the school children about Jesus Christ."

"If I cannot talk about my Lord, you might as well keep the contract," was my reply.

I went home that afternoon and told Arlene I had refused the contract for the next year. That night, we prayed, asking God for guidance and wisdom. The next day, I filed an application for a federal grant to return to graduate school for a degree in counseling and guidance.

We prayed for two weeks, asking God's leadership, and even daring to pray that He would lead us into the Pittsburgh-Youngstown area so we could participate in the ministry.

On April 17, a big, brown envelope was in my post office box. The letter had to do with my grant and began, "We are happy to inform you...." Not only was I going to be able to get my Master's Degree at Ohio University in Athens, only 250 miles from Youngstown, but the total amount of the grant and side benefits added up to far more than the school board in Conrad had offered.

You see, nothing is impossible with God! We are so prone to assess miracles by degrees. With God, there are no degrees where His power is concerned. The healing of multiple sclerosis is no more difficult for Him than providing for the toll bridge. Is this complex? No, it is simple. So simple that most folks miss it.

I missed it for thirty-three years!

7

Things are Different Now
by Donald Shaw

Donald Shaw holds a B.A. degree from Westmar College, LeMars, Iowa; a B.D. degree from Evangelical Theological Seminary, Naperville, Illinois and has done graduate work at New York Theological Seminary and State College of Iowa. Post-graduate work in Clinical Pastoral Training was completed at Kansas State Hospital, Osawatomie, Kansas, and Baptist Memorial Hospital in Kansas City, Missouri.

It all began in the summer of 1965. I had been going through what we ministers call a dry spell. I had been preaching every Sunday, but it was a powerless kind of preaching. There was little joy, little creativity, and little power. It had become pure drudgery. Saturday nights were almost nightmarish as I approached Sunday knowing it would be just another service as my parishioners and I sweated out another dull sermon. I dreaded seeing the sun come up on Sunday morning.

I guess you could compare it with a batter's slump that sometimes affects baseball players. Try as hard as I could, I could not seem to shake myself out of it.

As the hot summer days of July wore on, our vacation time arrived and my wife Pat and I arranged a trip to Red Feather Lakes in Colorado. We knew the children would enjoy it and it would give us a chance to stop over with my folks in Arnold, Nebraska. I had found that sometimes a vacation was the best thing that could happen to a minister. Just getting away from it all often helped. Besides, being around my home folks was always a tonic for my tired soul.

A few days after we arrived, Dad startled me a bit as I was finishing breakfast. "Don, why don't you pay a call to old Mr. Hartman before you leave," he said.

"Who is Mr. Hartman?" I asked as I put sugar into my second cup of coffee.

"He is a neighbor and a good friend of ours. He used to preach, but is now retired."

"Oh, I don't know," I answered, trying to find an excuse while sipping Mom's good coffee. "We are supposed to leave this noon for Colorado. Where does he live?"

"Right down the street," Dad said with an unexpected bit of determination. "It will only take a few minutes to walk down and see him." Against my wishes, I broke away from the leisurely visit around the breakfast table and headed down the shady street to the old frame house about a block and a half away.

It was a beautiful July morning. Even nature seemed alive with expectancy. The Hartman house was small and weary looking. As I approached, I saw him in his garden with a spade in hand, digging potatoes. A small pail was bout half full of scrawny, pathetic-looking potatoes. He was a small, white-haired man of ancient vintage and his face was drenched in perspiration. His long-sleeved, blue shirt was spotted with darker patches of moisture as the hot Nebraska sun beat down on his bent, moving figure. I cleared my throat and spoke, "Mr. Hartman?"

He looked up, wincing in the bright morning sunlight to see who had called him. I moved toward the edge of the well-spaded potato patch. He saw me coming and straightened up, wiping his wet brow with the back of his shirt sleeve in one motion.

"Mr. Hartman, I am Donald Shaw," I said, wondering whether he would recognize my name.

"Come over here and let me shake your hand, son," he said. "I have been wanting to meet you ever since I heard your Dad talk about you. You are the Presbyterian preacher, aren't you?" Even in that bright sunlight, there seemed to be a supernatural joy that beamed from his face. His eyes seemed to sparkle with energy and vitality.

Glancing down at his pail of tiny potatoes and then back at his face, I saw that his potato crop had not been all that might be desired. The potato crop in Arnold that year had been declared a total failure. Even the most venerable of the Arnold gardeners shook their heads gravely as they sat on the old timers' bench discussing the blight. But Mr. Hartman seemed blithely unaware of his crisis. He was digging potatoes and praising God at the same time. I wondered how he could be so happy.

What is his source of contentment, I asked myself. Here he is, living in a run-down old house all by himself. His potato crop is an obvious failure. He is out in the broiling sun, dripping wet with perspiration and bent with age, yet he is one of the happiest persons I have ever met. I had no answer to my questions.

Immediately, he began to talk to me about the Lord and about God's blessings on his life. Then, raising his eyes from the hard dirt of the potato patch and glancing around, he began to quote from the Nineteenth Psalm:

> The heavens declare the glory of God: and the firmament showeth his handiwork. Day unto day uttereth speech and night unto night showeth knowledge. There is no speech or language where their voice is not heard. Their line is gone out through all the earth, and their words to the end of the world. In them he hath set a tabernacle for the sun....

I was pondering over the possible meaning of this strange paradox in the potato patch when I was again arrested by his words:

> His going forth is from the end of heaven and his circuit unto the ends of it: and there is nothing hid from the heat thereof.

What a strange man, I thought to myself.

The conversation moved to my church and my pending plans to take a leave of absence and go back to school to complete my training in clinical pastoral care.

He was interested and said, "Come inside for a moment, Donald; I have something I want to show you." I followed as he moved toward the house, knocking the dirt off his spade and leaning it against the ancient wooden steps that led to the back porch. "Follow me," he said as he pulled himself up the steps toward the old, weathered screen door.

Inside the dark, plainly furnished house, we went to the living room where he began to fumble with the latch of an old trunk. It looked much like a treasure chest that had come from a Spanish galleon, and it had an aura of a "holy of holies" as he slowly lifted the creaking lid.

"Here is my latest growing edge," he said, smiling as he ruffled through a stack of quite new and up-to-date books. I noticed books by well-known writers. Very gently, almost reverently, he picked up *I Believe in Miracles* and handed it to me. "There is a great frontier these days in the healing ministry. While you are studying Freudian analysis and psychiatric medicine, I hope you will also open your mind to spiritual healing."

I glanced through the book with skepticism. The preface was written by a well-known judge and the dust jacket gave me some indication about the scope of the Kuhlman ministry. But who was Kathryn Kuhlman? Why all this enthusiasm? The whole idea seemed as strange as this prophet of the potato patch.

Time passed quickly and before I realized it, it was almost noon. "I must be going," I said. "The children are anxious to get to the mountains and we are leaving right after lunch."

Walking back up the tree-lined street, my thoughts lingered on the idea of spiritual healing. This had been one area which I had avoided like the plague during seminary days. Many times I had heard tales of those who had used it to accomplish their own selfish ends. Yet another part of me yearned to know more about all this, especially since I was preparing for a move into the field of clinical pastoral care. Maybe there was more.

I had been trained in the scientific method and wanted to know a great deal more about that book. Was Kathryn Kuhlman really an authority on miracles? Was spiritual healing authentic? I had many unanswered questions.

After returning to Conrad, we began to carry out our program for the new church year. There were the Conrad Hospitality Days and our eldest son, Mark, was busy building a float. We were also preparing to celebrate the eighty-fifth anniversary of our church. Things were active, as usual, but I had the vague feeling that church programs, study groups, and other good things were at the helm, and Christ was somehow left standing outside. I sensed that others, like myself, wanted to let Him in but simply did not know how to open the door.

Two weeks later I was in Waterloo on business and stopped by the public library. Out of curiosity, I checked to see if Miss Kuhlman's book was on the shelves. To my surprise I found it and decided to check it out. Returning home, I started reading—slowly, cautiously. I was approaching this new frontier as a critic. I also began to read other books on healing ministries.

I learned to my amazement that even some of the greatest psychologists were men of faith. For example, Carl G. Jung once said:

> The truly religious person...knows that God has brought all sorts of strange and inconceivable things to pass, and seeks in the most curious ways to enter a man's heart. He, therefore, senses in everyone the unseen presence of the divine will...If the doctor wishes to help a human being, he must accept him as he is. And he can do this in reality only when he has already seen and accepted himself as he is...Healing may be called a religious problem.

My interest was increasing.

In our young adult Sunday school class, we were studying the Book of Acts. Although my interest in healing was primarily academic at the time, I shared some of my interests with the group. There was some cautious response, but some were outspoken in their rejection of the whole idea. I realized I did not have enough information to speak with authority and again read Miss Kuhlman's book, as well as books on spiritual healing by Don Gross and Emily Gardiner Neal.

I had thought I was fairly well-versed and prepared in those fields relating to the established church's ministry. I had read many books in the field of psychiatry and clinical pastoral care as well as theology. My sermons were filled with quotes from well-known psychiatric and psychological writers.

In other words, I thought I had all the tools necessary for a successful, twentieth-century ministry. As I read, I began to wonder about my knowledge. Was it enough? A whole new area of ministry was unfolding before my eyes. Where had I been all my life? I had a hard time reconciling the idea of miracles of healing with what I had been taught, for all I had learned was completely contrary to any such idea. But it was difficult to refute the testimony of those who had been healed spiritually.

By nature, I was a skeptic, having grown up in a very intellectual and skeptical family. We had always prided ourselves on our education. I felt honored that I was being considered as a student at one of the best psychiatric training centers in America. This barrier of my cultural and intellectual background was difficult to eradicate.

About the time school was out in 1966, we began to make serious plans to accept an offer to move to the Kansas City area where I would begin my year's clinical work in pastoral care. I planned to serve one of the hospitals as a chaplain and member of the psychiatric team while I did graduate work in the clinical care program.

However, two weeks before we left, I had to make a trip to Waterloo to return some books to the library. After checking them in, I had a strange urge to head back into the stacks. That is odd, I thought. I came here to return books, not to look for more to read. However, I searched through the stacks where the books were kept and by habit found myself walking in front of the books marked Religion.

There it was again. The title simply leaped at me from the shelf (I Believe in Miracles.) What is God trying to say to me? I wondered half aloud. I took the book down and turned it around in my hands. Then I was hit by another urge. Check the book out and take it home.

"What?" I almost said it aloud for sure that time. I had already read this book twice. Besides, I was moving out of the state in less than two weeks. What was the need for the book? I had no answers, only a strong leading to take it home with me. So, shaking my head at my own foolishness, I returned to the front desk and checked it out. Now what caused me to do a foolish thing like that, I wondered as I walked down the worn front steps to my car. I was to find out the very next day.

It was late evening; my neighbor had been clipping his hedge and the street was strewn with trimmings. We were joking back and forth rather loudly when I looked up and saw Harold Selby coming down the sidewalk, limping along bravely on his two canes. I forgot my frivolity as I thought of the tragic waste of life surrounding this once-vibrant young man who had been struck down by the great crippler, multiple sclerosis.

In a town the size of Conrad you know most of the people. But we had just moved into the new manse and I had only met Harold once or twice. "Hi, Harold," I called out.

He smiled. It was a genuine smile in spite of the pain. We chatted for a few moments and I noticed he kept struggling to focus his eyes as we kidded with my neighbor about his adventures in landscape gardening. In a few minutes Harold moved on. I felt a sudden surge of pity for this man, so crippled, so hopeless, so in pain.

"Harold! Wait just a minute. Wait there a second, will you? I have something I want to give you." I dashed in the house and picked up *I Believe in Miracles* and returned to where he was waiting on the sidewalk.

"This may seem a bit irrational, I know, but I feel led to share this book with you and your wife. There is much about this that is still new to me. If you have trouble reading, perhaps Arlene can read it to you," I said. There was an evident eagerness on his part as he accepted the book. He shuffled on toward his house.

Several evenings later he was back, talking about the book. We stood on my back patio while he said, "Don, I have read those case histories and I believe them. Why can't things like that happen at home if people have faith and really pray to God?"

"I don't understand it, either," I said. "Maybe there is some kind of power that is released within a group that is filled with expectancy and faith. I wish I knew. Frankly, it is still a bit of a puzzle to me." I paused, half embarrassed to say what had to come next. "By the way,

I will have to ask you to return the book to the Waterloo library. We are moving next week."

Our new parish at Greeley, Kansas, was only twelve miles from Osawatomie State Hospital complex where I served as one of two chaplains in the new Adair branch hospital. The work was fascinating. Adair, like the other three hospitals of the huge complex, used the Menninger pattern of milieu therapy. There I experienced a kindness and compassion among team members that filled my work with real meaning. Physicians, psychologists and other team members had a genuine respect for the Christian faith, and patients were encouraged to hold onto those aspects that were positive and life-affirming. Our chaplain supervisors were men of unfailing patience and good will. I often sensed Christ's presence more among these broken bits of humanity in the state hospital than I did among the wealthy suburban socialites who crowded the fashionable churches.

Since our chance encounter at Cedar Falls Bible Conference in Waterloo, I had not heard from the Selbys. It was while I was in the midst of training that Pat and I received a letter from Arlene telling of Harold's miraculous healing back in Pittsburgh. I was amazed. I could hardly believe it. Yet I could not possibly doubt Harold's integrity. The question uppermost in my mind at that time was, will it last?

In the meantime, Harold had enrolled as a graduate student at Ohio University and invited me to visit him during his spring quarter holiday to look into some job openings. I agreed to come, but there was something else I was seeking—something even more basic in my spiritual life. True, I had been a Christian for years, but I sensed there must be a dimension of joy, enthusiasm, and power for service that I needed very much.

How could I preach faith when my own faith had grown so very thin? I remembered reading from Dr. Samuel Shoemaker, "If you want faith, go where faith is." Maybe this was what was drawing me to visit Harold. I could not fully account for the enthusiasm and steady optimism that came through so clearly in the letters we had received from them. I had been a Christian longer than either of them. I had studied both theology and the latest on Christian psychology. But here I was, so lacking in the one basic which underlay it all—faith.

"I cannot share with my congregation that which is not real to me," I told Pat one morning. "If God is breaking through in some new areas as Harold has described, then I must go and find out for myself. Not only do I want to see Harold, but I must attend one of these miracle services for myself."

This was the reason that the following Friday I walked up the steps of Carnegie Hall in Pittsburgh. I found myself standing in the midst of an expectant, mixed multitude. Many had been waiting nearly two hours. Poor and rich, upper, lower, and middle class, educated and uneducated, all blended together to make a truly ecumenical multitude.

One of those waiting on the steps was Dr. Thomas Asirvatham, a distinguished surgeon from a well-known eye hospital in Dindigul, South India. He was in the United States doing some graduate study. He was convinced that this movement was the work of the Holy Spirit. If a man of this stature believes, I thought, then why should I be so filled with doubt?

The service began and I watched in astonishment as the people joined in praising their God with joy and thanksgiving. There seemed to be a Presence which literally pervaded the atmosphere. This Something did not lend itself to analysis. It just seemed to saturate those present with agape love, joy, expectancy, and gladness.

"Dear Lord, whatever you have for me, I want it," I prayed. Then I added, "But, O God, if you do, please do it in a good, sane, quiet, respectable way. No emotion. No testimonies from me!" As the service progressed, however, my prayer changed. "Lord, whatever You want, I am willing. Do it Your own way."

Then it happened. It seemed that God's love came down and saturated every atom of my being. I experienced new faith, new hope, new life. The place seemed filled with the glory of God. I sensed something of what John must have felt when he was "in the Spirit" on the Lord's Day and described the brightness of the Presence of Christ. Whatever happened, it was as if a pilot light had been kindled in a cold, dead Presbyterian minister, and I suddenly tasted the fullness of the new wine of the Holy Spirit. I had previously known of the Comforter referred to in the Greek as the "paracletos." I had taught that He is with the Christian but all do not have His fullness. My prior experiences led me to believe that He was with me only as the sun is with us on a cloudy day. But now the clouds were rolled back and the reality of the sunshine broke through, and all things suddenly became bright and new.

Before returning home, I attended another of these Kathryn Kuhlman services. This one was held in the First Presbyterian Church in downtown Pittsburgh. There was the same note of happy expectancy, hope, eagerness, and faith. I met the pastor of that great church and we shared our amazement at how the Spirit of the Living God was manifesting himself in these days.

The big change in my life is the way the Scriptures have come alive. It is, of course, the same Bible from which I had always preached, but now it is different. It is different because the Spirit who inspired those who wrote it is now inspiring me anew to love and understand it. I am learning, even yet, that the Word of the Lord is revealed "not by might, nor by power, but by My Spirit, saith the Lord of hosts."

I wrote Miss Kuhlman a letter—maybe it sums up the whole thing better than anything else I could say:

> I hope you will ever continue on in the ministry just as you are doing now, and that you will never permit yourself to be sad or discouraged by the coldness of some of the clergy who scoff at faith and miracles and the Christ who turned water into wine. These skeptics are perhaps well meaning, but in their blindness they do that which is more fantastic still; they turn wine into water. They take the blessed wine of miracles, of revelation, of Holy Spirit manifestation, and turn it into the "water" of humanism, Sabellianism, and the ever present Pelagianism which permeates so much of the theology of our present day.
>
> One more thing. Do you realize, Miss Kuhlman, that through the anointing and the power of the Holy Spirit, you have succeeded in a measure doing precisely that which modern day, secular psychotherapy often attempts to do, but sometimes fails? Your ministry has succeeded in attaining the healing of the emotions.

Dr. Robert White of Harvard University, who wrote the text book used by our graduate school on Abnormal Psychology, describes psychotherapy as a "corrective emotional experience." Do you realize that through your ministry you have often accomplished exactly this? Through the Holy Spirit, you not only deal with the negative emotions of fear, resentment, worry, and despair; but there is a special Presence which becomes a veritable dynamo of compassion, tenderness, deep settled peace, infinite joy, gentleness, goodness, and a special kind of praise and adoration of the blessed Saviour, Jesus Christ.

Our modern day churches are filled with many good people (good in the usual sense of the word) who are terrified at the thought of emotion in religion. I think it was Clovis Chappel who once told us he had heard a minister of a very sophisticated congregation warning these people of the "dangers of emotion in religion." And yet, Chappel said, "I observed that the pews in which they were sitting were more emotional than the people."

How tragic that we humans, in our humanness, tend to fear the very Power that will heal.

8

When the Bough Breaks
by Dora Lutz

*The first time I met Dora and Joe Lutz was in
O'Neil's Department Store in Akron, Ohio when I
was autographing my book I Believe in Miracles. The
young couple shyly stepped forward and the lovely,
blonde wife smiled and said, "We just wanted to come
and tell you how much you have meant to Joe and
me"—and then her eyes filled with tears.*

*There was little conversation because of the crowd
standing around—but oh, I shall never forget the clasp
of her hand and the look on the young husband's face.
It was not until later that I found out why they had
come.*

Dora will tell you—just as she told it to me later.

It was just four days before Christmas and the last
present was wrapped and carefully hidden in the basement. A light snow was falling across the Ohio countryside and Joe glanced out the kitchen window as he
gulped his off-to-work cup of coffee. He said, "It looks
like a white Christmas for sure, honey."

I moved across the room and stood with my arm around his waist as we both drank in the beautiful scene through the window. The rolling fairways of the golf course behind the house were covered with a soft blanket of pure white. A gentle snow drifted down and collected on the limbs and boughs of the spruce pines that stood outside the window.

I gently squeezed his waist. "How about another cup of coffee?"

"Got to run, honey," Joe said as he began to pull on his coat. "Weather like this means lots of work for television repairmen." He kissed me on the cheek and started for the door when we heard the boys coming down the stairs.

It was their first day home from school on Christmas vacation. Mikie, eight years of energy and enthusiasm, came running into the kitchen and jumped on a chair as he reached for Joe's neck. "Daddy, Daddy, take me to work with you."

Joe leaned over and playfully patted him on the bottom. "Daddy has a busy day ahead, son; maybe you can go another time."

"But Daddy, I don't have to go to school today."

"I know," Joe said, "but not this morning. Don't you want me to get all my work done so I can stay home with you on Christmas?"

"Yippee!!" Mikie shouted. "Lemme give you a kiss so you can hurry up and get back." Joe reached over and Mikie kissed his cheek with a resounding smack.

Just then we heard Stevie, our ten year old, hollering from upstairs. "Wait for me, Daddy," he shouted, "I've got something I want to show you before you leave."

Joe looked at me and raised an eyebrow. "What's he got? I've got to get started," he said.

"He's been working on his big Civil War puzzle since yesterday," I said. "I guess he's finally finished it and wants you to see it before you leave."

Joe started into the front room when he heard Stevie start down the steps. "Hey, hold it," he shouted. "You can't bring that big thing down here. You'll mess it all up."

"But Daddy, I want you to see it."

"Well, just stay right there." Joe grinned and dropped his coat on the arm of the sofa as he said, "It's easier for Daddy to come up than it is for you to come down." Joe bounded up the steps and moments later was back down, pulling on his coat and heading for the door.

"See you tonight," he said. And the door closed behind him.

There were a million last minute things to do—baking, cleaning, and decorating. The boys had just swallowed their last mouthful of breakfast when there was a pounding on the back door. Several of the neighborhood kids, bundled up in their heavy coats with caps pulled down over their ears and scarves around their chins, stood in the drive. Stevie and Mikie ran to the door and peered out. "Be out in a minute," they shouted, running back into the house for their coats and gloves. "Man, I bet that's good sliding in the driveway today," I heard them saying as they struggled to get dressed.

I opened the back door and let them out and then stood momentarily looking through the glass storm door as they began running from the garage toward the sidewalk, slipping and sliding down the incline on their bottoms. I closed the inner door and busied myself in the kitchen. They'll be back in shortly, I mused. It's too cold for them to stay out long.

I was humming Christmas carols as I finished the breakfast dishes and mixed up some cookie batter. Twenty minutes later, just as I was sliding the first batch of cookies in the hot oven, the doorbell rang. Wiping my hands on the apron, I went to the front door, still humming under my breath.

A neighbor stood there, her coat hastily pulled over her housecoat and her head wrapped in a bandanna to cover the hair curlers. Her face was white and stricken and she stuttered as she talked. "D-D-Dora, something's happened." Her words escaped with little puffs of steam from her mouth.

I caught my breath, unaware of the cold air that whipped around me and into the warm house. "What's wrong?"

She had difficulty getting out the words. "Two boys," she said, "fell in the pond. I think they're your boys."

I stood in stunned disbelief. "No!" I exclaimed. "They can't be. They're right out here sliding in the driveway." My heart leaped into my throat as I looked toward the drive...it was empty.

"Get your coat," she said. "I'll show you where."

Somehow I managed to get back in the house, grab my coat, and stumble out the door. I hesitated. "There's no pond around here," I said. "You're mistaken."

"There's a big pond just beyond the golf course fairway," she said. "Haven't you ever been over there?" I shook my head as we started running across the frozen golf course.

"It can't be them," I kept saying to myself. "Dear God, please don't let it be them."

We ran to the top of a small hill and there, spread out before me, was a huge, frozen pond. I stood with my hand to my mouth as I looked at the horror scene below. A crowd of people had gathered on this side of the ice. Two police cars with flashing lights were parked close to the water. I saw two men dressed in dark rubber suits with skin-diving apparatus strapped to their backs bending over and pulling on their rubber flippers.

Then I raised my eyes and that dark, murky hole in the surface of the ice peered up at me...like the eye of death. Two sets of tiny footprints ended at the edge of the gaping hole. I saw their playmates huddled together near one of the police cars and I knew it was Stevie and Mikie under that ice.

I wanted to scream. I felt I was losing my mind. It's a dream...a nightmare, I thought. I'll wake up in a second and it'll be gone. But I knew I wouldn't wake up. I knew it wouldn't go away. I knew it was real and I couldn't stand it.

Joe and I were both Catholics, but our spiritual life was void. We had no real faith in God and only attended church because it was required of us. However, almost ten years before, I had started to listen to Kathryn Kuhlman's radio broadcast. Joe was aggravated because I grew to love the program, and several times had threatened to smash the radio if I kept listening to "that woman preacher."

I had heard that voice five times a week for the last ten years. But I never knew how much of an impact her preaching had made on me until that day on top of that hill overlooking that frozen lake. I wanted to run down the hill and throw myself in the icy water with my babies, but was stopped by that voice, her voice, saying, "Be still and know that I am God."

I stopped dead in my tracks. I felt what I recognized at once as the power of God come over me. God himself had used Miss Kuhlman's voice to speak to me in that time of heart-sinking terror.

Friends helped me back across the snow covered fairway to our small home. By the time I got home, the house was filling with people. A local Protestant minister had arrived and friends and neighbors were hurrying over. All wanted to help, but no one knew quite what to do. Police and then newspaper reporters arrived. The house seemed to be bursting with people and I felt the old panic returning. "Please, somebody call Joe," I said.

"We already have," someone answered.

Again I heard Miss Kuhlman's voice say, "As long as God is still on His Throne and hears and answers prayer, everything will turn out all right."

"Oh, I wish I could believe that," I said out loud. "I do believe it. I must. I have no other hope." I went into the bedroom and shut the door. Then I heard the faint wailing of a siren...they had found one of the boys. In my mind's eye, I pictured them pulling the small, frozen body up through that hole with little ice-encrusted mittens—the ones with the little ducks on the backs—flopping lifelessly back into the water. I saw those long, silky eyelashes, now glazed shut in death.

I fell to my knees beside the bed. "Dear Jesus," I sobbed, "please carry this burden for me. I can't do it." As I prayed, I felt great peace. Suddenly, I straightened up. What is happening to me, I thought. I should be going insane, but instead I'm so calm.

I felt a flow of energy surging through my body. It was an enormous strength. I was so strong, I could have lifted the house. I had linked my littleness—my nothingness—with His Greatness. "No matter what happens, you will never go down in defeat if you are linked to Jesus," I heard that familiar voice say again.

Suddenly the door burst open. I turned and saw that Joe was gripping the doorknob, his knuckles bone white and his face lifeless with fear. His lips, blue with cold and fright, moved wordlessly.

Dear God, how much he looked like Stevie! I wanted to reach out and draw him to me—to tell him everything was all right. Instead, I calmly said, "It's the boys...."

"Are they all right?" he screamed frantically.

"No," came my quiet reply. "They've drowned."

Joe turned and ran through the door. I wondered if he had heard that siren...if he had passed the ambulance on his way across town...what had been his thoughts as he drove up in front of the house to find it full of people...what agony was he now enduring?

I followed him into the living room in time to see him shove the minister against the wall. "I don't want any minister," Joe screamed, "I want my boys." He stumbled across the room, his body wracked in convulsive sobs, and collapsed on a couch.

The young priest from our church arrived. He thanked the minister and told him he would handle things. Moving toward Joe, he hesitated and then put his hand on his shoulder. "They do not prepare us for this in the seminary," he said weakly.

Joe was crushed, brokenhearted, lost. I knew he didn't know a single verse of Scripture or Bible promise. All he knew was the Lord's Prayer and Hail Mary. That was not enough at this time and I knew it.

God had given me a double portion of His strength to meet the needs of the hour. I could not believe it was me. There were many things to be done. Someone must identify the children. Someone had to make the funeral arrangements. Someone had to answer the reporters' questions. Someone had to talk to the police. God granted me the strength to do it all with calmness and sanity.

Joe was sitting on the sofa, crying and wringing his hands. His brother-in-law was trying to comfort him, but he was incoherent and almost delirious.

The police gave me the details. Mikie had fallen through the ice and Stevie, seeing him disappear into the icy water, had run to his aid, crying out, "My brother!" When he got to the hole, the ice broke and swallowed him up with Mikie. The pond was thirty feet deep. It took them almost an hour to find both bodies.

A neighbor took us to the hospital to make identification of the boys. Joe collapsed in the hospital corridor and had to be given medication. I stayed by his side while the neighbor viewed the bodies and made positive identification.

When we arrived home the funeral director met us at the door. Once again, I felt as if I were outside myself, looking on as an objective yet invisible outsider while this ninety-eight pound body of mine functioned flawlessly. I remember hearing Joe say, "God! What is holding her up?" Little did he know it *was* God.

Joe staggered into the kitchen and began pouring himself shot after shot of whisky. My Mom and Dad arrived and seeing Joe's condition, Dad wisely hid his hunting guns. While I sat on the sofa talking with the funeral director, Joe wandered aimlessly from room to room as if looking for something. He was totally unable to accept what had happened.

The next morning the cars from the funeral home arrived. They were ready for us to go with them to see our sons. It was terribly cold, with snow flurries blowing around the car as we pulled into the driveway at the funeral chapel. The directors urged us to go on in and view the boys before the friends arrived.

This was the hardest part—to see them like this.

Again I felt this great strength flowing through me, over me, around me. I knew it was Jesus. Michael, eight years old with dark hair, was on the right side of the room. Stephen, ten years old and with oh-so-blond hair, was on the left. I walked over to Stevie and put my hand on his shoulder. Again I heard Miss Kuhlman's voice talking about the death of her own beloved Papa. "It looks like him," she had said, "but it is only the shell." I looked up and thanked Jesus for His presence with me. I felt His great love and compassion around me and could literally feel Him weeping with me.

I walked over to Mikie. He was lying in an identical white casket. We always bought two of everything for them. I looked at Joe who was standing beside me, his face etched in grief. He was trying to speak. I could see his lips moving, but no words came out. I stood close to him, hugging his arm with both hands. "What is it, honey?" I whispered.

"Whatever it takes to get me where they are, I'll do it," he sobbed. "They're so innocent...." And then, for the first time in all our married life, I heard Joe pray. "Oh God, make me as innocent in your sight as these little boys. I want to go where they are."

Suddenly, Joe's last words to Stevie on that morning before he left the house flashed through my mind. "It's easier for Daddy to come up than it is for you to come down." Perhaps, I thought, this is what it's going to take for both of us.

The days that followed were full of shadows. The funeral was Saturday at St. Matthew's Church, followed by the burial service in the freezing wind. Walking back into the kitchen, I gazed at the little gifts the boys had made at school, still on the countertop where they had carefully put them the morning they died. "To the best Mom and Dad in the world...."

The shadows deepened and turned to night. Christmas floated past and then New Year's Eve. Joe had always gone out and whooped it up, but this year he sat home in the silent house and cried in the darkness.

Everything in the house was full of memories: the empty chairs at the dinner table; the rumpled clothes in the bottom of the closet; the drawers filled with little-boy underwear and mismatched socks. Things like rocks, bottle caps, empty shotgun shells, and children's books seemed everywhere in the house.

Then came that first day of school in the new year when I had to go to their classroom and clean out their desks. Their pencils, their scribbled papers, their workbooks, Mikie's big box of crayons...that's all there was left.

But there were memories; oh, the memories. That afternoon, I was standing in the living room when I heard the school bus stop in the street outside the house. The sounds of children laughing and shouting as they scattered to their homes cut into my heart like a sharp knife. I rushed to the windows and pulled the draperies, trying to shut out the sound of the frolicking children. I could almost hear Stevie and Mikie coming up the drive, swinging their lunch boxes and throwing snowballs at each other.

But on the third day that I pulled the drapes shut, I heard that same radio voice whispering, so softly, "It is not what happens to you that counts; it is what you do with what you have left."

"Thank you, God," I breathed, and opened the drapes, determined to rise above my grief.

It was not so with Joe. He cried all the time. He was unable to return to work. He couldn't sleep. He couldn't eat. He couldn't even dress himself. All he did was walk through that lonely house, wringing his hands and crying. At the breakfast table, he would break into uncontrollable sobs. He was losing weight, and he was chain-smoking himself to death.

I tried to get him to listen to Miss Kuhlman's daily radio broadcast, but his mind was too ravaged with grief to understand. Sometimes he'd sit at the table and try to listen, but would break out in great sobs in the middle of the program. I was deeply concerned about him, for it was as though he had completely lost his direction in life.

His hair began to fall out. He looked horrible, with his sunken cheeks and blood-shot eyes. Then, to cap it all, came the boils. Like Job of the Bible, his body was covered with the huge, agonizing sores. No one can imagine the torture and turmoil that badgered his body and grief-stricken mind.

He resigned his position as vice-president of the Television Technicians Association and threatened to sell his business, even going so far as to advertise it in the trade journals. He had lost all incentive to work, laugh, even live.

It was weeks and weeks before he was able to drag himself back on the job. Then one afternoon the mailman, a chap Joe knew only slightly, stopped by the shop on his rounds. He expressed sympathy over Joe's loss and then said a very strange thing to him. "Mr. Lutz, are you trusting in the Lord?"

At first Joe was insulted, then embarrassed. But he saw the obvious sincerity on the part of the mailman and answered, "Yes, I'm closely related to the church."

"I didn't say the church," the little mailman said kindly, "I asked if you were trusting in Jesus."

It hit Joe like a ton of bricks. This was the first time in all his life anyone had ever separated the church from Jesus. This was the first time he had ever heard that the two might be different.

Joe came home that afternoon and told me what an impression this had made on him. The priest had been by several days earlier and suggested we pray to our dead children for comfort. The Protestant minister had stopped, and in answer to Joe's question of "What can we do?" had suggested we read the twenty-third Psalm. "It's comforting," he had said.

But now, for the first time, somebody suggested we try Jesus Christ. Joe began talking to the mailman every morning as he made his routine deliveries. One day, he brought Joe a Gospel of John. Again, Joe was impressed.

That night I heard him rummaging around in the attic. "What are you doing, Joe?" I hollered at him, afraid he might be getting ready to shoot himself. "What's going on up there?"

Moments later he descended with an old Bible under his arm. "I knew we had one someplace," he said. "That radio preacher lady of yours says if you stick with the Bible, you can't go wrong. So, I'm going to start reading it." His voice broke and he began to sob, "If there's anything I can do to go to my boys, then I'm willing to do it."

So he began his intensive search, a search which was to lead down one blind alley after another until he emerged into the sunlight on the other side of the valley of the shadow.

Joe was getting up every morning and leaving the house early to attend Mass at St. Matthew's. He was listening to every radio preacher who bombarded the airwaves. He even followed up on some of the radio preachers and went to their offices where they prayed for him. He left no stone unturned in his search for God. Then one night, several months later, I told him I had finally broken down and written Kathryn Kuhlman a letter.

"What did you write?" he asked.

"I told her how she had been with me during the darkest hours of my life," I answered truthfully, "and that her life for Christ had given me a new hope."

"Maybe you've got a new hope," Joe said, his eyes filling with the ever-present tears, "but I have nothing."

I tried to comfort him, but he got up from the table and walked back into the living room. "Do you know what happened to me this afternoon?" he asked, pacing the floor. "I was driving down the street and started to cry. I had to pull off the road. All I can do is cry. Yesterday while I was fixing a lady's TV, I found a little toy dump truck under the set. I began to cry right there. All I want to do is see...see...my boys," he sobbed out. "It's all I can think about."

Two weeks later Joe came home from work and said, "Guess what? Your preacher lady is going to be at O'Neil's Department Store tomorrow to autograph a book she's written. Let's go see her."

I could hardly believe my ears. Kathryn Kuhlman was going to be in Akron. And Joe, my husband Joe, who had one time threatened to smash the radio, was asking me to go with him to see her. We got there early, but the line already extended out into the street. We stood watching her autograph the books. I couldn't get my eyes off her. She was so vibrant, so radiant, so full of joy.

Then we were next. We introduced ourselves and I said, "Maybe you don't remember, but I wrote you a letter several weeks ago and told you how much you had blessed us after our boys drowned."

"Oh," she said, rising from the table. "Of course I remember. I have been praying for you. How could I forget that wonderful, touching letter!"

Then, before we could reply, she put one hand on my head and the other on Joe's shoulder and began to pray out loud—right there in the middle of O'Neil's Department Store. She prayed for our salvation and for the Holy Spirit to descend on us.

As we walked out of the store, Joe's face was radiant. He put his arm around my shoulder and said, "Honey, Sunday we're going down and hear that lady preach in Youngstown. Maybe this is the answer to all my prayers."

Joe got up early the next Sunday and went to early Mass as usual. Then he came back by the house and we drove to the service in Youngstown. After that first service, we knew that if there was an answer to our spiritual search, it would be found under Kathryn Kuhlman's ministry.

We kept attending the Kuhlman services in Youngstown. I began to notice a change taking place in Joe. He stopped smoking. And then one day when I was upstairs, I heard banging and scraping in the basement. I looked out the window and Joe was dragging his home-made bar out into the driveway. By the time I got down-stairs he had set it on fire. We stood silently and watched it burn.

Several times after the services Joe turned to me and said, "I almost answered the altar call today, but some-thing keeps holding me back."

In March, 1963, fifteen months after we had lost Mikie and Stevie, whatever it was that was holding Joe back turned loose. We were standing side by side during the altar call when Joe turned and said, "I am ready. Will you go with me?" I hugged his arm as we stepped out in the aisle and started forward. I could hear Joe weep-ing as we walked down that long aisle and joined the crowd at the front of the auditorium.

We stood as close to the platform as we could and I heard Joe sob out, "Jesus, I am sorry." And no one will ever know the joy that swept my soul at that moment. I could feel Joe as he was born all over again into a new life, and I was being born with him.

Then I felt a soft hand on my shoulder and looked up to see Miss Kuhlman with that ever-present smile, urging us to come forward to the microphone. I do not know to this day how she remembered us or even saw us in that huge crowd. But she urged us forward and we stood before the microphone. "Why did you come forward?" she said, looking at Joe.

"Miss Kuhlman," he answered, his voice cracking but strong, "I have to see my boys again. I just have to be ready so I can be with my sons again."

"You can see your sons," she said. "You can be with them through all eternity if you will give your heart to Jesus. For that is where they are, with Jesus."

I gripped Joe's arm so tightly I was afraid I would cut off the circulation as he turned to those five thousand people and said, "Today, I take Jesus as my Saviour." Oh, the glory came down that day!

Since that time, Joe has been used by the Lord to win thirteen members of his family to faith in Jesus Christ, including his ailing father who went forward just a few weeks ago. All my family has come to Christ. And now, several years later, the teen-age boys who live in our neighborhood—former playmates of Stevie and Mikie—are gathering at our house for Bible study and going with us to the services in Youngstown. They pile into Joe's truck and go all over the city to worship and witness.

Most glorious of all, we have been used by the Holy Spirit to counsel with more than one hundred couples who have lost children through death.

Just recently, we stumbled across a passage of Scripture that wraps all our desires and all God's promises into one package. It is 2 Samuel 12:23. King David's infant son had died and David had ceased his mourning and said with assurance, "But now he is dead...could I bring him back again? No, I shall go to him; but he will not come back to me." And I remembered those words so seemingly incidental and yet so prophetic at the time: "It is easier for Daddy to come up than it is for you to come down."

Not only easier, but far more glorious!

9

It Could Happen to Your Daughter
by Charles Wood

There is no man so poor as he who has ONLY MONEY—and no gratitude! The Charles Wood family are just about the richest people in the world. They are rich in gratitude to God, for He did a wonderful thing for their daughter Sheryl.

Charles Wood is a member of the American Institute of Certified Public Accountants and is presently comptroller for a large Cleveland corporation.

In the fall of 1962, Sheryl, our older daughter, was an active, athletic thirteen-year old girl who had just entered the eighth grade at Olmsted Falls Junior High School. The summer before, she and Carol, her eleven-year-old sister, had attended a Christian camp and participated in a full list of activities ranging from baseball to pillow fights. Now Sheryl was trying out as a cheerleader. Every afternoon our backyard was the scene of cartwheels and flips, as cries of "rah-rah-rah!" and "block that kick!" bounced off the walls of our house and others. The fact that Sheryl's activities had caused her several hard licks on the head did not seem too important at the time. It was all part of being a vital, fun-loving teenager.

Then, one Monday morning, my wife Gwen received a phone call from the school office saying Sheryl had fainted in the hallway. Gwen rushed to the school. By the time she arrived, Sheryl had fully recovered, but Gwen took her home. The next day, however, Sheryl was back in school. On Wednesday, a call from the school secretary reached my office. Sheryl had fainted again and they had been unable to get in touch with her mother. I left the office at once and drove to the school. A little pale and quite frightened, Sheryl seemed all right otherwise. However, I made an appointment with our family doctor for that afternoon.

Finding no cause for alarm after examining Sheryl, the doctor thought it would be safe to let her return to school. He suggested that we call him if Sheryl had further difficulties. The very next day I received another call from the school. Sheryl had fainted for the third time. They had been unable to revive her and she had been taken to the Southwest Community Hospital in Berea for emergency treatment.

I rushed to the hospital and was relieved to find that Sheryl had already regained consciousness. I insisted, however, that she be admitted as a patient. When she had fainted, her head had struck the tile floor and the doctor suggested we have X-rays taken of her skull. This was done, and a spinal tap also, in an attempt to determine the reason for the fainting spells.

Because the tests were inconclusive, the doctors suggested a few days rest and further observation in the hospital. During her hospitalization, Sheryl had still another fainting spell, this time while seated in a wheelchair.

Eventually, although there still was no firm diagnosis, she was allowed to return home and resume school attendance. Within the next several weeks she had many more fainting spells and complained of a "ringing" in her head. One day she reported that when she and some of the kids had stuck each other with pins, she could not feel the pin pricks on her right arm.

Sheryl's fainting spells grew more frequent and she remained unconscious for longer periods of time. It was becoming increasingly difficult for her to keep up with her school work—not because of the absences, but because of the "ringing" in her head of which she complained more each day. Late one night I was awakened by her moaning and crying. Stumbling to her room, I found her holding her head and twisting back and forth on the bed. "My head, Daddy, it feels like it is going to burst open."

The only thing that seemed to relieve the pressure was the blaring noise of the radio. By blaring, I mean so loud that not one of the rest of the family could sleep. Sheryl would go to sleep with her little radio going full blast. Later, I would slip into her room and turn the radio down so the rest of us could get some rest.

Finally, during the first week in November, we made an appointment for Sheryl to begin a series of tests as an outpatient at the Cleveland Clinic. I watched the first tests as the doctor took a needle and gently ran it back and forth across her forehead. She could feel it on the left side but not on the right. The same testing was done on her stomach and the soles of her feet with similar reactions. Seemingly, she had lost most of the reflexes on the entire right side of her body. We also learned that she was developing double vision and that the hearing in the right ear was being impaired. Her facial features were beginning to change as her right eyelid began drooping over her eye.

By mid-November, her headaches had become so severe that we had to keep her home as many as three days at a time during the week. She was losing strength as well. Then, Friday night before Thanksgiving, Gwen and I were preparing for bed when we heard a dull "thump" in Sheryl's room. We rushed in and found her inert body lying at the foot of her bed.

My heart was in my throat as I picked her up and tried to revive her without success. Nothing we did brought her back to consciousness. My anxiety was surpassed only by my frustration and hopelessness in the situation. I put her on her bed and bent my head to pray. When I looked up, I saw Carol standing in the doorway, her childish face pale with fear and her eyes wide with horror. "Dear God, why does she have to see this?" I moaned.

That night Sheryl was admitted at the clinic as an emergency case. Our trip home was depressing and our whole world seemed to be falling apart. Neither Gwen nor I slept much the rest of the night and in the next room I could hear Carol's soft whimpers as she sobbed in her sleep.

"Please God, do something. Help us, please," I prayed.

The next morning about eleven o'clock, a doctor from the clinic called. "Sheryl is all right," he said, "but this morning she got out of bed and fainted again, hitting her shoulder as she fell. We X-rayed it and the pictures show the right arm is broken about an inch below the shoulder and the bone in her right shoulder is chipped. You can see her after lunch, but I wanted you to know you would find her in a cast and sling."

What is happening, I asked myself as I hung up the phone. Everything was going so smoothly and now it is all going wrong. As a deacon and treasurer of our church, I was definitely spiritually-oriented, but this was more than I was prepared for. I could sense something was horribly wrong, yet I felt totally helpless in the face of it. Gwen called our pastor. He was kind and sympathetic and came to the house to pray with us.

Carol, however, decided to take more positive action. That afternoon while Gwen and I were visiting Sheryl at the clinic, she wrote a letter. Unknown to us, she had listened occasionally to Kathryn Kuhlman on the radio. Sensing our anxiety and knowing that something was wrong with her big sister, she sat down and wrote out a prayer request to Miss Kuhlman. While we were gone, she walked the mile and a half to the post office and mailed it.

Three days later the doctor called us and said they had taken new X-rays of Sheryl's arm. The new pictures indicated that the arm had not been broken at all, only badly bruised. The only possible explanation, he concluded, was that a technician had misread the first X-ray. However, the coincidence of the prayer request and now the healed arm caused Gwen to begin to give serious consideration to the probability of spiritual healing. It was the beginning of what was to be an entirely new way of life for all of us.

Sheryl stayed in the Cleveland Clinic for two weeks. They had run a full battery of tests including electroencephalograms (brain wave tests). The tests indicated that a part of her brain was not functioning in a normal manner under certain given conditions. This was the cause of the fainting spells. They were still hesitant about making a diagnosis, but, for the first time, I heard the doctors using the word "seizures." Before leaving the clinic, Sheryl was given medicine which was supposed to cut down on the number and the intensity of the seizures. She was advised to go to school as much as she was able.

However, the seizures continued and each time they seemed to last a little longer. The school officials were most sympathetic and understanding, and the principal even assigned one of her close friends to stay with her and watch over her. The dangers associated with Sheryl's condition were painfully evident, and we realized after the fall in the hospital that she should never be left alone. We tried to watch her when she went up and down the steps at the house, but this was not always possible. Gwen still had meals to fix, housework to do, and I still had to go to my job. Constant anxiety settled upon our daily lives.

Just before Christmas, while Gwen and Sheryl were shopping in the big Zayre's Department Store, Sheryl fainted. She was rushed to Fairview Park Hospital in the Fire Department ambulance, but was dismissed after emergency treatment. Although we somehow managed to get through the Christmas holidays, there was always a dark, foreboding cloud of the unknown hovering over everything that used to be bright and cheery.

Each day seemed to bring new reasons for discouragement and further despair. We now noticed the seizures were becoming more violent and their frequency was increasing. Sometimes Sheryl would go several days without fainting—other times she would pass out several times in one day. When she returned to school after the holidays, it became an accepted act that she would probably have a seizure before the day was over, often right at her desk.

"Surely," I said to Gwen late one night after we had sat up with Sheryl, "there must be some place where we can get help." That night we prayed a humble, sincere prayer for divine help.

In January, I heard about a doctor who had had good success treating patients with similar conditions. We checked and found he was one of the most respected neurologists in the Cleveland area. We called and made an appointment.

After a series of examinations, the doctor called us in for consultation. "Sheryl seems to have had an injury to the left side of her head in the section of the brain that controls the reflexes on her right side. However, there is no doubt that our diagnosis of epilepsy is correct." I couldn't believe my ears. Epilepsy! And not only was it epilepsy, but the doctor said it was the Grand Mal variety, the most serious type.

The doctor was encouraging and said he could almost guarantee that the seizures could be reduced to no more than two a year through the use of drugs. This was the first encouragement we had had and we went home willing to face the future bravely and wait for the drugs to perform their promised miracles.

We learned a great deal about epilepsy during the next several months. For one thing, we learned that there is a certain amount of electrical current that flows through the brain, much the same way electricity passes through the wiring of a house. If there is some kind of injury to the wiring, it will often cause a short circuit and blow a fuse. In the same way, if there is an injury to the brain, under certain conditions it can cause a short circuit in the brain's electrical system—resulting in a seizure.

We also learned that almost ninety-five percent of the cases of epilepsy are caused by injury to the brain—either at birth or later in life. Suddenly, that series of bumps on the head that Sheryl had received the previous summer and fall grew increasingly important. Any one or all of them could have caused her present disability.

At the present time, there is no cure for epilepsy. In rare instances, an operation on the brain can relieve the condition, but even this will not bring about a cure. "It can be arrested," the doctor counseled, "but never cured."

He also warned that precautions should be taken to protect her from further falls, which could prove to be fatal. We were advised to prohibit all activities such as swimming, bicycle riding, and other sports. Since even the exertion of playing her clarinet often brought on a seizure, she would no longer be able to play in the school band. So Sheryl's once active and athletic world was circumscribed by restrictions and enforced inactivity. High-spirited adolescence gave way to sedentary routine.

But her seizures continued, taking on frightening aspects. At first she had fainted quietly; now she would clench her fists and thrash her arms and legs convulsively when the attacks began. Often I would have to force her jaws open to pry her tongue from between her teeth. Even in limited activities, there seemed to be danger. Hearing about one young person who drowned in a bathtub during a seizure increased our anguish.

Sheryl's hearing was another source of anxiety after two ear specialists determined she had now lost sixty percent of the hearing in her right ear. By spring, we were averaging between two and three trips a week to various doctors. Then one of the drugs prescribed for

Sheryl had an adverse effect on her gums, which became swollen and began to grow over her teeth. Dental surgery would be required to remove the excess gum tissue.

Helplessly, we watched our daughter's decline as her appearance and actions changed. Her movements became sluggish and slow. The drugs often caused her to stagger like a drunken person and she would clutch a chair for support or lean again the wall while walking. Although our hearts ached, we tried to put up a brave front, not only for Sheryl's sake, but for Carol's. But deep inside we felt that all hope was being drained away.

I was desperate. I'm a Baptist deacon, I thought, active in every phase of my church's life, but I am powerless in the face of this. It never occurred to me to pray for divine healing. Miracles happened in biblical days, I had been taught, but not any more. Healing in our day was accomplished by doctors and nurses and "miracle" drugs. All this added to my frustration as I found myself praying to a God whom I thought no longer performed miracles such as we needed for Sheryl.

Gwen had begun listening to Kathryn Kuhlman on the radio occasionally. She had a sneaking suspicion that Sheryl's "broken arm" had been healed through the ministry of prayer. She tried to persuade me to listen, but women preachers just did not fit into my theology.

Most of my life I had been taught that women were not supposed to have authority to lead men. As a deacon, I had joined with the others in our church to make sure that no women achieved such status. When women missionaries visited our church, we went to considerable lengths to see that they did not occupy the pulpit, allowing them instead to speak to women's classes or give their testimonies.

I was also chairman of the Ohio Council of Evangelical Baptist Missions, and part of our task was to examine the prospective missionaries and make recommendations to various boards. One of the requirements we imposed was that women missionaries would not teach men on the foreign fields. Thus, when Gwen asked me if she could take Sheryl to a "healing service" in Pittsburgh conducted by a woman, I was reluctant to give my approval. I wanted nothing to do with "faith healers," especially women.

"I have heard of too many fakes," I demurred. However, Gwen pointed out that Miss Kuhlman made no claims to being a "healer." Disarmed by Gwen's persistence and Miss Kuhlman's disavowal of peculiar healing power, two weeks later when Gwen again asked if she could take Sheryl to a miracle service in Pittsburgh, I gave my reluctant approval. Gwen and the children were accompanied on the trip by Gwen's father and her sister Eunice.

After the service had started, Gwen's father said, "Don't you think you ought to take Sheryl down to the platform and have Miss Kuhlman pray for her?"

Gwen, uncertain of the order of the service, was hesitant. However, when Eunice pulled Sheryl by the arm and said, "Come on Sheryl, we are going down," Gwen consented. Halfway down the steps at the back of the auditorium, Sheryl turned and looked at her aunt with a strange, almost weird look.

"What's wrong, honey?" Eunice asked.

"I don't know," Sheryl said. "Something just popped in my ear. I can hear."

Although Eunice and Sheryl did not hear it, at that precise moment Miss Kuhlman was saying from the platform, "Somebody's ear has been opened." Gwen immediately thought of Sheryl. Desperately hoping it was, she was still shocked to see Miss Kuhlman come down off the platform and meet Sheryl and Eunice halfway down the aisle. Miss Kuhlman reached out and gently touched Sheryl's head. Immediately Sheryl collapsed to the floor under the power of God. Almost overcome with awe, Gwen met them in the lobby, tears of rejoicing streaming from her eyes.

Driving back to Cleveland, the little band of pilgrims were still elated. Over and over they spoke of what they had seen and heard. Sheryl's hearing was definitely restored and Carol seemed as enthused about it as her sister. That evening, Gwen said to me, "If God can do this, then surely He can heal her epilepsy as well." Yet, if another miracle was in store for Sheryl, we received no advance notice. That night she had another seizure.

"Chuck," Gwen said to me shortly thereafter, "Miss Kuhlman also holds a Sunday service in Youngstown. Why don't we drive down next Sunday?"

My responsibilities at the church and the press of other duties made it necessary for me to postpone the trip for almost two months. In the meantime, Sheryl's seizures grew much worse. Some of them lasted up to two hours and left her body in such a state of shock that her recovery was painfully slow. Moreover, we realized that not only had her body changed, but so had her personality. She was becoming highly rebellious, creating almost palpable tensions in our home. We hated to discipline Sheryl, for that could provoke another seizure. Yet we also had Carol to think of, and we could not let Sheryl have her way about everything. What could we do?

Nothing seemed to be right. Gwen's weariness and strain were obvious. Contrary to our hope, Sheryl's seizures had not been controlled by the medications. Our family life showed signs of breaking under stress. Nothing could have made this more plain than Gwen's admission to me that she had reached a stage where she would rather see Sheryl die than continue living in the poor health that seemed to be her destiny.

Just after Sheryl had reached her fourteenth birthday, a missionary conference was held at our church. At the close of the conference, I glanced up and saw my afflicted daughter coming forward to dedicate her life to the Lord's service. Watching her, I shook my head in pity. Poor child, I thought. What can she give God? What could God do with a deformed body, a damaged brain?

Sheryl virtually dropped out of school the last two weeks of the term. The seizures were now coming almost daily and their duration could not be predicted. Her teachers passed her, I think, mainly because they admired her spunk. We made plans to begin our vacation the second week in June. We would be going to our small cottage in the country, and I agreed to take a route that would allow a stop in Youngstown on the way. A week before we were to leave, Sheryl had her worst seizure. It was almost fatal.

It began around midnight on Saturday night. We had been sitting in the living room and Sheryl was on the sofa. Suddenly she jumped to her feet and said, "Oh, Daddy...." Then she stiffened. I rushed to prevent her from falling against the coffee table. Gwen helped me stretch her out on the sofa as her body went into one spasm after another. Every muscle in her body was tensed; her fists were closed so tightly, it was impossible to pry them open. It took every ounce of strength I possessed to pull her jaw down and force a wadded handkerchief between her clenched teeth. The seizure showed no signs of abating, so about 1:00 A.M. I finally called the neurologist. He told me to try to get some medicine into her. "If it doesn't work," he said, "bring her to the hospital and we will see if we can do something here."

Gwen and I sat at opposite ends of the sofa trying to hold Sheryl's writhing body. In time I managed to get a few pills down her throat, but the seizure continued for another hour as one convulsion followed another. "Oh, God," I prayed out loud in my desperation, "please help us."

Then almost as if I heard an audible voice, I remembered a passage from Jeremiah that Gwen and I had long cherished: "Call unto me, and I will answer thee and show thee great and mighty things, which thou knowest not" (Jeremiah 33:3).

A great peace swept over me as I recalled these words. I looked down on the writhing, twisting form of our young daughter and consciously committed her to the Lord's keeping. Moments later I sensed something taking place in her body. The convulsions ebbed and a peacefulness came over her face. She fell into a deep sleep.

I reached down, picked her up in my arms and carried her across the living room and up the stairs to her room. Gwen went before me to prepare the bed and we gently tucked Sheryl beneath the sheets.

That night I lay awake until the first streaks of rose-colored dawn lit the eastern sky. "...Great and mighty things which though knowest not...." The words whispered over and over again through my mind and strangely assured me.

A week later, on Sunday morning, we started our vacation. First we drove from Cleveland to Youngstown to attend the worship service conducted at the Stambaugh Auditorium by Kathryn Kuhlman. Because we were late arriving, Gwen and Carol ended up sitting in the balcony, although Sheryl and I found seats on the ground floor, three rows from the front.

The music was heavenly. There was something alive, something vital about the entire service. For the first time in my life I could actually feel the presence of the Spirit of God in a group of worshipers. We joined in the singing and then, about halfway through the service, Sheryl turned to me and said simply, "Daddy, I'm healed." Her voice was soft and confident. Her eyes glittered like sparkling stars on a winter night.

"How—how do you know?" I asked, stammering in disbelief.

"I don't know, Daddy," she whispered, "but it felt like something came down and took all the pressure off my head. The ringing has gone. My eyes don't hurt any more. My head doesn't hurt. I'm healed, Daddy, I know it. It was as though God put His finger on my head and took away all the hurt."

As I looked deep into her eyes, my own eyes began to fill with rare tears. I tried to talk, but could not. Leaning over, I pulled her close to me, embracing her in the presence of all those people. I was oblivious to those who turned to watch the little drama between father and daughter.

I suppose one of the workers sensed what was happening and told Miss Kuhlman, for when I looked up she was there beside us. Her whole face seemed to smile and her eyes sparkled. "Dear Jesus," she said softly, "from the bottom of our hearts, thanks!"

Still awed, we staggered to our feet. Miss Kuhlman gently touched Sheryl's cheek, and she dropped to the floor under the power of the Spirit. "This is a marvelous healing," Miss Kuhlman said to me. "God will use this girl as a testimony of His power."

And He has. My own faith has been greatly strengthened as well. I had come face to face with a miracle and knew that from that time forward my actions and reactions would be based on faith, as well as knowledge.

After the service we returned to the car and together we thanked God for what He had done. We agreed that the miracle we had shared must be accepted on faith.

We continued our vacation. More than twenty-four hours had passed since Sheryl's last seizure—the longest she had been free in months. The doctors had said that failure to give Sheryl her medicine could result in continual, eventually fatal, seizures. That afternoon she walked seven holes with me on the golf course. Any exertion, the doctors had warned, would bring on a seizure. Sheryl was weak and tired, but it was a healthy exhaustion. The next day, for the first time in almost a year, she went swimming. No seizure. I had no more doubts. She was healed! From that time, Sheryl has been completely surrendered to God's care and no medication, not a single drug, has been administered since that glorious day in Stambaugh Auditorium.

Later that summer, Sheryl returned to the same camp she had attended the summer before. She participated in all activities and won the outstanding girl camper award.

One year later, Sheryl entered Houghton Academy in New York where she competed and excelled in a variety of athletics: girls' football, basketball, and track. Competing against both college and high school students, she won seven ribbons at track meets.

The reader will appreciate, I am sure, the joy I take as a father in sharing with you an experience that is dearer to my heart than anything else that ever happened in my life. Gratitude is the hardest of all emotions to express. There are no words capable of conveying all that one feels. Until we reach a world where vocabulary knows no bounds, we have chosen to express our thankfulness to God by giving our lives to Him and telling people everywhere what He has done for our family!

10

A Doctor's Quest
by Robert S. Hoyt, M.D.

*Dr. Hoyt was born in Korea in 1925, the son of a
missionary surgeon. He holds degrees from the University of California (A.B. and M.D.) and took post-
doctoral studies in pathology at the University of
Cambridge in addition to specialty training at the University of California in San Francisco. He is a diplo-
mat of the American Board of Pathology.*

Late on a Sunday afternoon, in November of 1967, I
found myself standing on the stage of the San Francisco
Civic Auditorium at the end of an evangelistic meeting
with Kathryn Kuhlman. This was a strange place for a
medical doctor to be!

Many years of my life had been spent in medical
school and pre-medical education, followed by an intern-
ship and then five years of scientific training and studying the anatomical and physiological changes of the body
that occur in disease states. A pathologist is trained to
study the origin, nature and, with the aid of modern medical instrumentation, the progress of disease in the human
body.

Raised in a Christian missionary home, some of my earliest memories are of kneeling in our living room as we prayed for the needs of our family and the church. I claimed Jesus Christ as my Saviour during my teen years, and He carried me through many trials in military service during World War II in the Naval Air Force. After the war, I started pre-medical work and then entered medical school, but my witness was growing weaker and weaker. During my third year of post-doctoral training, a Christian doctor told me my Christian life was almost nonexistent. I am glad he did; it was a turning point in my life.

In 1965, I volunteered to go to Ethiopia for a year to establish a department of pathology at Haile Selassie I University. I went to satisfy my desire to serve God in my chosen field of medicine—as a non-professional medical missionary.

It was while I was in Africa that I came face to face with the reality of God's power. I was particularly impressed with a Roman Catholic sister, a missionary, whose great love and compassion for the sick overwhelmed me. I saw Sister Gabriel throw her arms around lepers, tuberculosis patients, and persons with horrible skin diseases. I had never seen a love like this in action and I began to realize just how empty and powerless my own life was. I began to yearn for God's love and power in my own life and committed myself to a deeper quest to find it than I ever had before.

During my year in Africa, I learned of the miraculous moving of the Holy Spirit in the Wallamo Province in the southwest part of Ethiopia. The details of this story, which took place during the Second World War, are found in *Fire on the Mountains* by Raymond Davis.

Three missionaries had gone into the Wallamo Province by mule-back (the only means of transportation at the time). It took them three years to learn the language and another year to win the hearts of thirty-five natives. Then the Italians invaded Ethiopia and the missionaries were driven out, leaving behind a pitifully small handful of native Christians. The only thing the missionaries left behind was a crude translation of the Gospel of John.

Five years later, one of the missionaries was allowed to return to Ethiopia for a visit. He kept hearing stories about a huge Christian movement in the Wallamo Province. After three months, he finally wrangled a way to visit in the southwest section of the nation and there found a church with more than ten thousand members. He was aghast. Entire villages of born-again Christians were scattered throughout the province—and, most impressive, were the tremendous testimonies of healing. People who had been blind were now seeing—cripples were now walking.

Apparently, when the missionaries translated the Gospel of John and then were forced to leave in such a hurry, they forgot to tell the natives that the day of miracles was past and that the miracles Jesus performed in the power of the Holy Spirit were impossible today! Those new Christians had read the Gospel, believed and prayed, and God had moved.

I believed the missionary records and testimonies of these miracles in Ethiopia and I returned to the United States amazed at the power of the Holy Spirit in modern times in Africa. I wondered why God did not move in this way in America.

During the next six months after my return home, I worked very hard in our hospital laboratory and continued some teaching. In my spare moments, I tried to secure new equipment and personnel for the laboratory we had started in Ethiopia. I felt a desperate need, seeking for more of God in my life. I knew there was a power that performed miracles, because I had heard of it first hand in Ethiopia; but where did one find such power in America?

Thinking perhaps missionaries might have the answer, I began reading one missionary biography after another. In a Christian bookstore one day, still searching for more biographies, I stumbled across John Sherrill's book *They Speak With Other Tongues*. I did not know the first thing about the infilling of the Holy Spirit until I read this account by this careful reporter of *Guideposts* magazine.

That night the Lord gave me faith to believe that He would move into my life in power as I prayed for the infilling or baptism of the Holy Spirit. I went to bed *believing* that I would be different the next day and when I awoke, it was a glorious morning. Heaven came down and glory filled my soul!

Jesus was so near, it was as if He were physically present, walking around the house and through the rooms. I suddenly found a great continuity of my life with His and with eternity. I had been really grafted into the "vine" and His love and power began to pour through me. I have never been the same since and that sense of the reality of Christ has grown stronger.

Soon thereafter, I heard of Kathryn Kuhlman and made plans to attend her service at the Memorial Temple on Nob Hill in San Francisco. There were many things that happened there that I simply could not explain from my medical knowledge of the ordinary disease processes. The only explanation is that there are laws of God higher than any of the known laws of science and medicine!

At the close of the Memorial Temple service, as we stood for the benediction, our attention was drawn to a father and his fourteen-year-old son coming down a side aisle toward the stage. From the expression on the father's face, it was hard to tell whether he was registering awe, fright, or unbelief. Then, quite unexpectedly, he began to weep unashamedly. As they came to the stage, the young lad handed Miss Kuhlman two hearing aids and said, "I can hear."

We stood motionless; not a sound disturbed the stillness. The father quickly told the story. He had been standing with his son in the top balcony when the boy turned to him and said, "Dad, I can hear." The boy pulled both hearing aids from his ears and said he could hear perfectly.

This was real—I knew it!

For the next several months, I attended most of the miracle services on the West Coast. Finally, I called Kathryn Kuhlman in Pittsburgh and said, "I am on my way to Pittsburgh. I want to personally examine and interview some of the people who have been healed by the power of God in years past." I had a feeling I was nearing the end of my quest.

I checked. I examined. I interviewed. I came away absolutely convinced that God is still performing miracles. I have been taken to a new echelon of faith in the living Christ through the ministry of Kathryn Kuhlman.

The greater miracle, however, is the changed life rather than the changed body. Surgeon's hands can transplant a heart, but not a life! I shall never forget the sight of hundreds of young people coming forward to enter into life and to live it more abundantly—coming forward by the score and standing on the stage of the Shrine Auditorium in Los Angeles, California, with 7,000 witnesses. Hands upraised, they were asking God to change and fill their lives.

There is a young couple whom I shall always remember, who stood on stage together while they repeated their marriage vows for the second time. There had been a separation because the tentacles of alcoholism had completely gripped this man. But in one of Kathryn Kuhlman's services, his life was transformed as he accepted Christ as his Saviour. His wife, cautious and understandably so, watched him for many months until finally, she also believed. Now they are a Christian family and he has taken his place as a respected and useful citizen in his community.

Dr. Alexis Carrel, Nobel Prize winner and first man to keep living tissue alive outside the human body, has summed up my own feelings in a beautiful paragraph from one of his books (*Voyage to Lourdes,* Harper: 1950):

> As a physician, I have seen men, after all other therapy failed, lifted out of disease and melancholy by the serene effort of prayer. It is the power in the world that seems to overcome the so-called "laws of nature." The occasions on which prayer has dramatically done this have been termed "miracles." But a constant, quieter miracle takes place hourly in the hearts of men and women who have discovered that prayer supplies them with a steady flow of sustaining power in their daily lives.

On another occasion, Dr. Carrel was confronted by the supernatural healing of a patient afflicted with tubercular peritonitis. He wrote:

> The wildly improbable became a simple fact. The fact that I can find no explanation for the cure disturbs me deeply—and it horrifies me. Either I must cease to believe in the soundness of our methods and admit that I am no longer able to diagnose a patient, or I must accept this thing as an entirely new, outstanding phenomenon which must be studied from every conceivable angle. Such cures cannot be brought about by natural means.

And even though Dr. Carrel did not complete his quest, he finished his writing with a simple prayer...a prayer which all medical doctors (and all others for that matter) should use as they continue their own quest:

> Thou didst answer my prayers by a blazing miracle. I am still blind to it. I still doubt. But the greatest desire of my life, my highest aspiration, is to believe, to believe passionately, implicitly, and never more analyze and doubt.

11

An Invalid the Rest of My Life
by Eugenia Sanderson

*San Diego, California, will never be the same since
the healing of Eugenia Sanderson. Neither will you
be the same after talking with her.*

*When we were making a telecast at CBS Televi-
sion City, Eugenia turned to me and said, "I want the
whole world to know what God has done for me—to
think, I would have been an invalid all my life were it
not for His tender mercy."*

*Miss Sanderson was head of the Dietary Depart-
ment at Cedars of Lebanon Hospital in Los Angeles
until 1955, when she accepted a similar position with
a large hospital in San Diego. She holds a B.S. Degree from Kansas State University and did intern
work in New York City. She is a member of the American Dietetic Association.*

The future looked bright when I left Cedars of Lebanon Hospital to accept the position as Director of Die-
tetics at a newly-opened hospital in San Diego. I had just
turned forty and my plan was to work there until I
reached retirement age.

Nine years later, that plan was interrupted when I became acutely ill. I was given a private room in the hospital and the doctors went to work trying to diagnose the strange symptoms of my illness.

After extensive tests, my condition still was not diagnosed. I returned to work, but the pain was so severe that my doctor arranged for me to be admitted to a large hospital in Los Angeles. There a diagnosis was made by a specialist—I had a rare disease called dermatomyositis. My doctor in San Diego checked the records and concurred with the diagnosis.

Dermatomyositis affects the nerve endings and causes severe pain in all the muscles, joints, and nerves—especially in the skin. I knew something of the symptoms and knew the prognosis was very gloomy. But I had no idea how intense the suffering would become as the disease progressed. Almost every muscle and nerve in my body was affected.

I was sent back to San Diego where I spent the next two months in the hospital. My diaphragm was so badly affected that for a while I required oxygen to breathe. Every treatment known to medical science was tried on me. Every time my doctors, who were so wonderful, heard of a new drug, they gave it to me. But nothing helped much. The pain grew worse and most of the joints in my body were swollen.

Our hospital staff is well known for its compassion and fine patient care. The nurses were my friends, for we had worked together for nine years. Several told me later how their hearts ached to see the suffering it caused me as they gently bathed me and tended my needs. One dear friend was praying I would die rather than have to continue to live in such pain.

Six months later, I was able to return to work, but by May, 1966, my condition had gradually worsened to the extent that my doctor, who is a compassionate Christian, arranged for me to retire from my position on a long-term disability. Then, as kindly as he could, he explained that medical science could offer no cure. I was sent home to live as an invalid.

For many years, I had shared an apartment with Viola Eberle, a dear personal friend who is a registered nurse. I knew she would be close by to minister to me.

During the next ten months, the pain grew so severe I could hardly stand it. My skin felt like a third-degree burn over parts of my body. Even the movement of my body across the bed sent waves of pain through my system. My muscles began to deteriorate.

Then I noticed the nerve endings in my sinus, tongue, and mouth had become irritated. The joints in my knees, elbows, hands, and feet were swelling. And my eyes...the nerve endings in my eyes were so sensitive that even a bright light caused pain.

Viola helped me arrange a frame to fit under the covers so none of the bedding could touch my body. Yet at times, my skin was so sensitive that it could not tolerate even the friction of a soft nightgown.

Sleep was almost impossible during this ten-month period and I was only able to nap throughout the long, endless hours. At one time I had been able to be up a couple of hours a day and perhaps even stand a short ride in the car, but as the condition worsened I found myself confined to my bed.

My eyes hurt so badly I couldn't even watch television, and reading was almost impossible. I spent my time with the draperies pulled and the door closed, my only comfort being the small transistor radio that I kept beside my bed. It was through this tiny black box that I had first heard the voice of Kathryn Kuhlman over XEMO in San Diego.

The music was wonderful and I found myself looking forward to the daily broadcasts. As the days wore on, I almost forgot the music as I listened to what she had to say. She was talking about the love of God, about the sick being healed, about miracles. And I began to get a glimmer of hope.

Much time was spent in intercessory prayer—the only way I could serve my Lord now. I had been reared in a Bible-oriented home back in Kansas. I had grown up loving the Lord and had taught a Sunday school class in the First Presbyterian Church of San Diego. I believed in a God Who could do anything.

But healing? As a member of the hospital team, I knew that God worked through doctors, nurses, hospitals, and drugs. I had never really considered divine healing in the twentieth century. But as I continued to listen, I began to think, perhaps there is a chance for me. Maybe, just maybe, the God I had loved so long was bigger than I realized. He was a God of miracles after all.

One day, I heard Miss Kuhlman mention her book, *I Believe in Miracles*. I called a local Christian bookstore and they graciously offered to deliver it to my home.

This marked a turning point in my life. The book was very difficult to read because of the pain in my eyes. It took me until February of 1967 to finish the book. By then I realized that my disease was progressing so rapidly that, within a month, I might have to be placed in a nursing home. I was taking twenty-five pills a day and the pain was growing more intense each day. My only relief came when I lay in a tub of hot water.

In looking back, I often wonder if God allowed the sickness of my body because it was in His plan for my life. I do not know, even now. But I do know that I had reached the stage of desperation. I would have done anything to ease the pain.

I heard on the radio that there were chartered buses that drove once a month from San Diego to the Kuhlman services at the Shrine Auditorium in Los Angeles. On an impulse, I made reservations for the next week. When Viola learned what I had done, she offered no encouragement. But she knew how desperate I was and helped me plan to go. Since she was unable to go with me, I asked my sixteen-year-old nephew Randy to make the trip.

Oh, how I dreaded that trip! But I had been praying all these months and had asked God to either heal me or call me home. And I had developed a deep feeling, after having listened to Miss Kuhlman's radio broadcasts, that God wanted me healed.

God only knows the terrific effort involved that Sunday morning as I got up and pulled on my clothes. As I dressed, I knew that the time had come to do the impossible. And I was going, even if it killed me.

But the worst was still to come. I had rented a wheelchair and Randy wheeled me to the door of the bus. I slowly stood to my feet and approached the steps. For months, it had been impossible to raise my legs high enough even to step on a curb. But I knew I had to get on that bus. I used the few muscles I could, but was unable to close my left hand to grasp the rail. The bus driver started to help me.

"Oh, please don't help me! Please don't touch me!" I cried out as he started to put his hand on my arm. It took long minutes of determination, but by slowly twisting and turning I was able to climb aboard. I still don't know how I did it. God was surely with me, helping all the way. They folded my wheelchair and stored it in the bus.

The woman I sat next to had been to the services at the Shrine before. She told me of the wonderful miracles she had witnessed and, despite the pain, my hopes soared. She told me about one of Miss Kuhlman's helpers, a woman who worked in the congregation during the healing service. She said she was often attracted to those who were being healed and would pray with them as their strength returned. "O Lord," I prayed silently, "please let this be my day."

I had brought my lunch with me, but was too weak to lift the thermos or even peel my banana. The kind lady next to me broke the skin on the banana and peeled it for me.

The bus had a flat tire halfway between San Diego and Los Angeles, and the delay caused us to be late in arriving. The meeting had already begun when we pulled up in front of the huge auditorium. I could hear the magnificent singing from the street. The building was jammed to capacity and hundreds of people were packed around the outside doors. My heart sank. I was still on the bus. All the others had gotten off and were escorted inside by an usher. Randy and I were directed to the wheelchair entrance at the side of the building. But those doors were locked; the auditorium was filled. Had I come all this distance and endured this pain only to be turned away because the crowd was too great?

My mind turned to the old, familiar Bible story of the man who had come to Jesus for healing—a person much like me. Just as it was today, the crowd had been too great. But four of his friends had carried him to the roof of the house and, removing the tiles, had lowered him down through the roof so he could be at the feet of Jesus. How well I remembered those ringing words of hope and life that I had read in my Bible, "Arise, take up thy couch, and go into thine house" (Luke 5:18-26).

"Oh, God," I prayed, "even if You have to let me down through the roof, please help me get inside."

Randy wheeled me to the front doors, but it was impossible to get through the mob of people. Inside, I could hear the marvelous singing, but I was outside with no way to enter. I remember looking at the roof, hundreds of feet above the busy street. I was willing. God knew that.

God had other plans that day. For just then a woman, a perfect stranger, stepped out of the crowd and said, "The Lord just spoke to my heart. You are to be healed today. This is your day." My heart leaped in my chest as she made her way through the crowd to one of the front doors and began to pound until it nearly came off the hinges.

Soon the door cracked open and an usher stuck his head out. I don't know what transpired, but the next thing I knew the crowd parted and I passed through like Moses through the waters of the Red Sea. Suddenly, I was inside.

The wheelchair section was filled to capacity. I saw dozens of crippled and lame persons straining to hear every word that was being spoken from the stage. Down on my left, a man got up and motioned me to a seat in the center section. I slipped out of the wheelchair and lowered myself into the seat. I was in so much pain and I felt so weak. I fumbled in my pocket and took out a pain pill. That was exactly 2:45 P.M. on February 26,

1967. I can be so precise about the hour and date because it was the last one I was ever to take.

I looked up and Miss Kuhlman was on the platform. The air was supercharged with spiritual power. She was preaching and every eye in that gigantic auditorium was fixed on her. Every heart beat with her heart.

I glanced around and saw I was in a section with several small children, some quite handicapped. Praying parents took turns holding them, their little heads falling back and forth. My heart ached for them and I turned my thoughts from friends for whom I was praying and began to pray for these small children. I felt I had lived a good productive life up until this last year. I was satisfied to die and go home to be with the Lord. But those children—oh, God, how my heart went out for them.

Then, without warning, I felt a touch on my shoulder. I remembered it because it was a normal touch, without the pain that usually accompanied any kind of pressure. I looked up and there stood a tall, dignified woman with gray hair. She leaned close to my ear and whispered, "How are you feeling?"

I had not thought of myself for those past moments and suddenly I realized that the pain was leaving my left eye. "I just noticed my left eye is better—it is different." I smiled, hoping this was the beginning of my miracle.

"Do you want to get up and walk?" she asked. I was completely surrendered to anything. All around me in the congregation, I could sense the healing power of God at work in other people, and now me.

I stood slowly to my feet, dizzy with excitement. "Walk up and down the aisle with me," the woman said with a gentle voice. "Just trust Jesus to heal your body." And then I was walking. Even with my limited medical knowledge, I knew the adrenaline was going full blast. But I knew there was something else at work in my body, also. I could sense I had been touched by the power of God himself.

The worker was helping me as I walked. She had hold of my arm, but there was no pain. I could feel the strength flowing back into my body like air being pumped into a deflated balloon. I thought of the persons I had seen returning to life in the hospital as they were given transfusions of blood. But there were no needles sticking into my arms. There was no transfusion of blood, only a transfusion of the inpouring power of the Holy Spirit.

I could lift my legs. The muscles were slowly gaining strength. We walked back and forth up the aisle. It seemed like we walked for miles. We stopped at the stairs to the platform and I stood there, listening to others who had been healed as they shared their testimonies. I was amazed that I was able to stand so long without pain. Suddenly, it was my turn to step forward.

"What is this? What is this?" Miss Kuhlman asked with excitement as I walked toward her. "Come tell the people what has happened to you."

I walked to the microphone and, before more than seven thousand people, testified of my condition and what had taken place as I sat in the audience.

"Praise God," Miss Kuhlman said as she put her arm around my shoulders. "Isn't Jesus wonderful?" I could only nod through the tears of rejoicing.

I turned to her and said, "It's still taking place. I can feel the power of God surging through my body."

"Walk with me," Miss Kuhlman said. I forgot the crowd. I forgot everything as I walked back and forth across the platform. Miss Kuhlman's face was aglow as she walked with me.

Turning back to the microphone, she put her hand into the air in a gesture of glee. "See, I had nothing to do with it. It was all the Holy Spirit. I do not even know this woman. I have never seen her before. She was healed without my knowledge. I did nothing. It was all God."

The congregation broke into spontaneous, tumultuous applause, and the organist struck the keyboard with a powerful refrain from the Doxology. "Keep walking! Keep walking," Miss Kuhlman was almost shouting. "Lift your legs higher. Lift them as high as you can."

I was walking! Back and forth across the front of the stage in front of all those people. I was pulling my knees almost up to my chin and slamming my feet down against the floor. From all over the auditorium, I could hear people saying "Praise God" and "Amen" and even from the choir and those on the platform. I could hear men and women saying, "Thank you, Jesus." Perfect strangers were rejoicing over my healing and thanking God. Oh, how I thanked Him, too!

I returned to the microphone and Miss Kuhlman, her face wreathed in smiles, her eyes glistening with tears, laid her hands on my head and prayed a prayer of thanksgiving. Suddenly, I was on my back on the floor. I had no idea how I got there, but I was stretched out full length on that hard wooden floor, having fallen under the power of the Holy Spirit. Equally amazing was the fact that my joints and skin, which minutes before were in such pain, were now relaxed and strong.

An usher helped me to my feet. I found my wheelchair on the way back down the aisle and pushed it ahead of me through the back door and out into the sunlight. I was the happiest person on earth.

I walked across the street to the bus. The warm California sunshine felt good and soothing on my skin. I climbed aboard the empty bus and took a seat. I could still hear the excitement from inside the auditorium as others were healed. But on the busy streets, the traffic roared as usual and people walked up and down the sidewalks, staring curiously at the auditorium and the mob of people still gathered around the outside doors. I knew someone else had already claimed my seat. "Thank You, Jesus," I whispered, "oh, thank You."

My mouth felt dry from all my praising God and I reached for my thermos. I effortlessly twisted the top. "I am healed!" I shouted to the empty bus. "I am healed!" I leaned over the seat beside me to raise a window. This act, too, was effortless. I sat back, laughing, remembering how the bus driver had struggled to raise that same window when he had our flat tire.

On the way back to San Diego, a festive spirit prevailed on the bus. Everyone was rejoicing, patting my back and clasping my hands. All this physical contact, I thought, and no pain...no pain.

Even those who had come and not been healed were rejoicing. It was almost more than I could stand. My nephew was as excited as I and he told everyone he had not seen his aunt look like this in more than three years.

When I arrived home that night, Viola met me at the door. She was almost panic-stricken since I had been gone so long. Now she saw me enter the door of the apartment, walking normally and my face sparkling with excitement. My dark circles were gone. I was a walking miracle. Thirteen hours before, my body had been full of pain. Now, I stood before her healed and whole.

161

She remained speechless as she watched me undress and examine myself. My joints were still swollen, but my muscles were much stronger and the pain—all of the pain—was gone. "I am still being healed," I told her. She just shook her head.

That night, I pulled the canopy frame off my bed and put on the first nightgown I had been able to wear in a week. We praised God together and then I crawled into bed—actually, I bounced into bed—and pulled the covers up snugly around my chin. That night, I slept soundly for the first time in almost a year. When I awakened the next morning, the excruciating pain which always had accompanied the first movement of muscles was gone. I felt wonderful.

Three weeks later, I attended the next service at the Shrine Auditorium. That day, sitting in the center section, I felt that same excitement and anticipation. Suddenly, I felt my shoes loosen and drop to the floor. I looked down at my stocking feet and saw the swelling had completely and instantly left my lower extremities. The healing was complete. All that was needed now was time for my natural strength to return.

I returned to my doctor a few days later. He was astonished to see me walk into his office and questioned me closely. He was happy, very happy, but also cautious in stating his opinion. I knew he was thinking I was in a state of remission and the old symptoms would soon return.

At his request, I returned several times for examination. On my last visit, he pronounced me totally cured and stated my healing could be classified under no other category than a miracle.

The most wonderful thing that happened to me was the change in my life. I am a new person—a changed person. I wake up singing. The sun always seems to be shining and my heart is constantly filled with praise and gratitude to the Lord for His tender mercy.

When my minister at the First Presbyterian Church heard of my miraculous healing, he called and asked me to testify before the church on Wednesday night. Since then, I have had opportunities to testify before many groups in the church and community.

It took a little more than a year for my strength to completely return so I could go back to work. However, I was afraid it would be impossible for me to return to the strenuous work in a Dietary Department. I had hired hundreds of people and knew I must prove to myself, my doctor, and my employer that I was able to produce the work required. So, as my strength returned, I went to work in our church office as a volunteer receptionist.

After several months, my doctor released me for work and I returned to the same hospital, this time as a therapeutic dietitian.

Only God could have made such a complete change. I give Him all the glory. And now, when I stand in my church on Sunday morning and sing, "Praise God from Whom all blessings flow," it comes from the bottom of my heart.

My friends look at me in amazement and wonderment and say, "I cannot believe it!"

I believe it. It has happened to me.

12

Portrait in Ebony

by Aaron Jacobs

His radiant smile made him a figure I shall never forget. He was almost in a state of ecstasy as he walked toward me and I knew something miraculous had happened!

An African, Aaron Jacobs, whose real name is Haruhah Yakubua, is an instructor of political science at Ahmadu Bello University in Zaria, Nigeria. In 1966, he was selected as one of two graduate students at the University of Nigeria to come to the USA on an Exchange Student Scholarship to study political science at the University of Pittsburgh. Shortly after returning to Nigeria, his wife Joanne gave birth to their son Emmanuel.

In 1901, the Sudan Interior Mission sent a man to the village of Patigi in Northern Nigeria to tell the Africans about Jesus Christ. That missionary, remembered only as Reverend Lang, took up his work among the villagers, most of whom were Moslem and all of whom were hostile. He was the only witness for Christ within hundreds of miles.

No one knows for sure how many years he labored in that unrewarding field before he returned to the States to die. It must have been a frustrating experience watching the seed fall on the unplowed ground of unreceptive hearts. My grandfather was one who found Christ through Reverend Lang's faithfulness to God in Nigeria.

My grandfather became a loyal messenger of the Gospel. Even though he died when I was only five years old, I can still vividly remember the frequent trips he took into the bush country to preach the message of salvation. He would come back with hair-raising stories of adventure among the bush people and the wild animals. Not only did my grandfather preach in the bush, he also witnessed at home. His entire family, including my father and uncle, became Christians.

It was the tradition in Nigeria at the time that the eldest son live with his uncle. So upon the death of my older brother, I inherited the responsibilities of the eldest son and left home to live on my uncle's farm on the outskirts of Patigi.

My uncle took great interest in me and saw to it that I enrolled at the University of Nigeria. There, enamored with the challenges and opportunities of Africa's emerging young nations, I majored in political science and won a scholarship to come to the United States to do graduate study at the University of Pittsburgh.

I was excited about coming to America, not just because of the academic opportunity, but because I had such a high opinion of the spiritual life in America. The missionaries who had followed Reverend Lang had been deeply spiritual people. They had taught me about Jesus

Christ and had ministered ably to the spiritual needs of my family. Thus, I naturally assumed that all Americans were like the missionaries. It was with great anticipation that I looked forward to coming to the great land of America to fellowship with the millions of deeply spiritual Christians who lived here.

The day my wife Joanne and I arrived in the United States was the happiest day of our lives.

As a political science major, I had studied the progress of this nation from its very beginning. I knew the stories of the founding fathers, the pilgrims, who came to these shores to escape religious persecution and worship in freedom and truth. I had studied the documents which make up the foundation of the nation's government—the Declaration of Independence, the Constitution, the Gettysburg Address, and the inauguration addresses of many of the Presidents.

I had read of the great halls of learning which supposedly gave bold recognition to divine authority and I was impressed with the slogan "In God We Trust" which was engraved on American coins. I had read of America's great preachers—I knew that many of the great universities were first founded as divinity schools and seminaries to teach young preachers. How eager I was to come and study in such a Christian atmosphere! It would be the next thing to heaven.

What I did not know was that America had drifted far from her spiritual moorings. Freedom had degenerated to license, and the secular was honored over the sacred. Materialism, sensuality, and immorality had become a prime way of life. I soon discovered a sophistication born of a desire to discover natural explanations for all phenomena which had resulted in the humanizing of God and the deifying of man. I found few Godly foundations and little Christian fellowship. My dreams and hopes were dashed against the flinty rocks of agnosticism and atheism.

In fact, nothing was the way I expected it to be. Most of my professors and those around me were just not the type of people I thought I would meet in America—and they certainly were not like the missionaries I had known in Africa. Christ was neither accepted nor honored. Immorality flourished in the open and the churches seemed more like mausoleums than centers of worship of the living God. I felt spiritually isolated. In short, I was a most disappointed fellow.

Why had the missionaries not warned me about all this? I yearned to return to Africa, for unregenerate man is just as spiritually blind in a prosperous and academically enlightened nation as he is on a jungle trail in a remote and primitive culture. If I am to be around heathens, I thought, I would rather be around heathens at home. Sometimes I prayed, "God, why did You allow me to come to this land?"

God knew what He was doing, even when I did not. I wrote my missionary friends in Africa and told them of my great disappointment. Shortly afterward, I received a visit from a Christian man in Pittsburgh. He had been contacted by the missionaries and asked to come see me. Just to know there was someone who cared made things better.

About this time, a lady gave Joanne a copy of *I Believe in Miracles*. She read it and was impressed. "This might be a wonderful place for us to go," she said, referring to the miracle services at Carnegie Hall.

I had serious reservations. For eight months, I objected to Joanne's urgings to attend the miracle services. However, I finally agreed to go. Perhaps I could find that vitality which was lacking in my spiritual life. Believe me, I did.

Halfway through the service, Miss Kuhlman pointed directly at our section and said, "There are two people in that section who are being healed right now. One of them has a back injury. Take your healing in the name of Jesus."

Suddenly I remembered. It had been with me so long that I had grown accustomed to it. In 1954, I had injured my back in a soccer match in Nigeria. For fourteen years I had been in and out of clinics seeking some kind of remedy for the constant pain. The doctors had told me I would just have to learn to live with it and although I was never without pain, I had grown accustomed to its constant presence. I had not even thought of it until Miss Kuhlman said someone had been healed.

This is ridiculous—there is no such thing as spontaneous healing. Yet I cannot possibly be just imagining that something is happening to me, I thought. It was a strange heat in my spine. No, I kept telling myself, it cannot possibly be the power of God—it must be a form of hypnosis.

Miss Kuhlman kept saying, "There is someone in the balcony to my left who has received a spine healing."

Finally I could resist no longer. It was as if a voice kept saying, "It is you. It is you. The Lord has healed you." And before I knew it, I was on my feet walking toward the stage. The pain that had been my constant companion all those years was gone.

I now understand that the only way the Lord could prove Himself to me was by touching my body. He knew my first contact had been with unbelievers. He knew how disappointed I was. He knew I was discouraged, empty, sick. I now feel that the Lord brought me to this country and let me go through my disappointments specifically for this one experience. For not only was my back healed, but I received a brand new perspective of the power of God.

Now I am back in Nigeria, teaching in the Department of Public Administration at Ahmadu Bello University. My people need more than political science. In this war-torn land where brother is fighting against brother and mercenary soldiers are killing for money, I am convinced that only the power of God can save us.

There are thousands, millions, who have never heard. If only Kathryn Kuhlman could come to our country—to our people. They need what she has to offer—Jesus Christ! Even if she cannot come, I have promised my Lord that I will follow in the footsteps of my grandfather and carry the Gospel of Good News of Jesus Christ to my people. It is their only hope and security.

13

Things Money Cannot Buy
by Carol Zenallis

It is my firm conviction that the greatest miracle in the world is the transformation of a life.

At one time, George Zenallis owned and operated the biggest and most expensive night clubs in Akron, Ohio. He was nationally known for the big name stars who performed on his stages. He is one of the most likable and affable men that I know, and one can easily understand why George Shearing stayed after hours in the club just to entertain George and the rest of the boys.

Carol Zenallis, his pretty wife, tells how, through her illness, she and George found God.

It started back many years before when national Prohibition was first repealed. George was one of the first to obtain a liquor license. He opened a restaurant and bar called "The Brass Rail" on Whiskey Alley in Canton. Four years later, he sold it at a profit and with two other men bought out "Bender's Tavern" in Massillon. It became known from coast to coast as a famous restaurant.

Later, he bought "The Giant Cafe" and then the "Old Mill" and the "Yankee Inn" in Akron.

Across the years, he had rounded up and put under contract the best entertainers in show business. There was Ted Mack and his band for a fall opening in Canton. Traveling with him were the Andrew Sisters. All the top names were waiting for an opportunity to play his clubs: Count Basie, Artie Shaw, Tony Bennett, Mel Torme, George Shearing. He was "big time" in the field of night club entertainment.

Then there was Johnny Ray. He came in one evening looking for a job. George bought him a topcoat, paid his room rent at a hotel, and hired him at seventy-five dollars a week to play the piano. Later, when Johnny was making ten thousand dollars a week and more, he would still come back to Akron and play George's clubs. It reminded him of the old days.

George bragged that his clubs were the top two liquor buyers in the city. In the eyes of the public, he was a success, but I wanted him out of the liquor business more than anything in the world. It was wrecking our home life. It is difficult to be in the liquor business and not drink—George was drinking at least a fifth a day. He drank with everybody. "If you don't drink with the customers, they get mad," he said. "And you cannot afford to make enemies in the cocktail business." The fact that he was losing me did not seem to matter.

One night a violent storm was raging as I turned into our driveway. The power lines had been torn down by the hard winds and the torrential rain was so heavy, I almost missed the house. Yes, house was the right word because it takes two to make a home and all I had was the children.

Immediately, the children were taken up to their bedrooms and tucked in and I hoped they would not sense my fear. I was always in a constant grip of fear when left alone, and the electrical storm terrified me even more. Going back down the stairs, I could hear the house groaning and creaking as it struggled to stand against the surging wind. One could actually hear the nails screeching out of the boards and shingles.

Petrified, I dialed the phone and asked for George. I was afraid of dying. "Please, honey," I begged him, my voice shaking with fear, "please come home and be with us." There was silence on the other end except for the background music and the laughter of those near him at the bar.

Finally I heard him say, "There is nothing to be afraid of. Who is afraid of a little wind? If danger comes, you and the kids get down in the basement and get under that heavy steel table."

"Please...," I pleaded and a sudden flash of lightning broke the phone connection.

The house shuddered as I crept into my room to spend the night alone. Standing in the middle of the bedroom, shivering with fright as the lightning made weird reflections on the draperies, I felt like the loneliest person in the whole world. There was no one to turn to—no one. In my desperation I dropped to my knees, "Oh, *Theoma*," I prayed (calling Him by the Greek word I had used as a child—the word for "my God"), "I don't know if You are listening to me. I hope You are. Please protect us."

Suddenly I remembered my childhood and the many happy times spent at a little Christian mission in Cleveland. I could remember the preacher saying, "When you are saved, you know you are saved." What does "saved" mean, I asked myself.

My prayer continued. *"Theoma,* teach me what it means to be saved. Please lead us to a place where we can be taught this together. Please help us—help me."

Getting up from my knees, I remembered my Bible. I reached into the night stand for it and with shaking fingers opened the flyleaf and saw the date: 1932. It was the year I had attended the Christian mission in Cleveland. Suddenly, I realized it was the first time since we had been married, almost eleven years, that the Bible had been opened.

"Please, my God," I cried out, "forgive me." A strange calmness and peace came over me, and while the storm raged outside the house, I crawled into bed and prayed once again, asking God to show me where to read. The Bible fell open to the Book of Revelation and chapter after chapter moved beneath my fingers as I turned the pages in fascination.

I do not know how long I read, but I finally laid the Bible beside me and got up and stood at the window. Outside, during the vivid flashes of lightning, I could see the tall poplars bending from the frightening force of the wind. But the fear of the storm had left me. There was a new kind of fear—a fear of what was to come.

"Please, my God," I whispered through the rain-streaked window, "bring George home. Please, my God, bring him home to stay."

As the days went by, an amazing hunger for the Bible developed in me. In the mornings, after George had gone to work and the children had left for school, I would sit at the kitchen table and read. The stories seemed so fascinating and God's teachings were so marvelous. When I ran across a particularly meaningful passage, I would mark it in red and ask the Lord to let me experience it.

One day I was visiting with my mother, a devout Greek Orthodox. "Carol," she said, "there is a woman on the radio who really knows the Bible. You should listen to her. She teaches the truth."

"What is her name?" I asked.

"Kathryn Kuhlman." I did not know it at the time, but this was the next step in God's answer to my prayer.

The following morning, I was ironing in the kitchen when I remembered Mother's suggestion. I turned on the radio and picked up the voice of Kathryn Kuhlman—a voice which was to become my constant friend and spiritual advisor.

Morning after morning, I read my Bible and listened to her. Always, Miss Kuhlman would begin her broadcast by saying, "No matter what happens to you, no matter what your problems are, as long as God is still on His Throne and hears and answers prayer, and just so long as your faith in Him is still intact, everything will come out all right."

So I turned to Him—*Theoma*—my God. I read about Him. I talked to Him. I let Him talk to me through His Word. He was changing my life.

But there was one thing about my life that remained unchanged—my health. As a young woman, I had been seriously injured in an accident which had left me with a bad curvature of the spine. As the years passed, it grew worse and with the birth of my children I gradually became deformed. My left hip was two inches higher than my right one and my shoulder blades protruded. My back and shoulders were stiff and I could not move my head without swinging my shoulders also. Sometimes the pain was so excruciating, I could hardly stand it.

Then came the final blow. The joints in my body began to swell—knuckles, wrists, knees, ankles—all movement was becoming painful. After a period of time, the pain grew so severe I could not close either hand. We finally made an appointment at the Akron Clinic where I had a complete examination.

The doctor called us both in and gave us the results of his examination. "Rheumatoid arthritis," he said shaking his head. Then turning to George he said, "She will never get well. My own wife is a patient here at the Clinic with the same condition—confined to a wheelchair."

"What are you trying to say?" George stammered. "Isn't there something you can do?"

"I am saying that barring a miracle, your wife will be just like mine in a relatively short time."

We stood there stunned. In my heart, I was resigned to live or die in God's hands. But George was still grasping, searching for some cure. "Please, doctor," he said, "money is of no consequence. Can't you do anything for my wife?"

The doctor's sharp eyes cut into George's world of financial make-believe. "Let me level with you," he said. "All the money in the world cannot buy your wife's health. It is gone. All we can do is try to relieve the pain."

I was shocked, but in that moment I felt a deep sense of pity for George. He had never faced a problem like this. Always before, he would have been able to buy his way out of trouble. But this time, it was different. I read the emotions that flashed across his handsome Greek features: anger, fear, and finally despair. My heart cried for him more than it did for me. In the midst of all his big-time friends, famous entertainers, flashy showgirls, and big money—George actually had nothing. Nothing.

This confrontation with reality had shaken him to the core. I thought the doctor's diagnosis would soften him, but instead it seemed to harden him toward God. He became more and more involved in his business. As for me, at least I had God!

I could hardly wait to get home so I could take my Bible and get alone to pray. Reading the Bible lifted me up and thrilled me. How fortunate these people were to be healed by Jesus.

Early one morning, George joined my mother and me as we sat in the kitchen listening to the Kathryn Kuhlman broadcast. She was describing a woman from Massillon who actually had been healed of cancer. If God can heal her, He can heal me, too, I thought. I looked across the table at George and then glanced at Mom. "I am not going to have that operation on my spine," I said, referring to the doctor's suggestion that surgery might help my condition. "God will heal me."

George just gave me a blank stare!

I had definitely changed, but the change was not in my body, which grew progressively worse. The change was in my attitude. I had more patience, compassion, understanding. And even though the hell of George's life sometimes crushed in on me until I thought my heart would break, I still loved him, and I fasted and prayed for him constantly.

I will never forget the first sign of change I saw in George. He called one day from the club. "Your preacher lady is going to be in town next week," he said. "I thought you would like to try to go to one of her meetings."

"Kathryn Kuhlman? In Akron? George, are you sure?"

"Yes," he said. "I read about it in tonight's paper. Of course I cannot go, but I thought you would like to take the children. Maybe your mother will go with you."

It was too wonderful to comprehend. Not only that I would be able to hear Miss Kuhlman speak in person, but that George had actually called and told me about it. It was a big step for George.

"Thank You, *Theoma*. Oh, thank You, my God," I prayed.

Something happened to me during Miss Kuhlman's meetings in Akron. I sensed a completeness, a satisfaction in my spiritual life I had never felt before. Listening to the music, seeing the miracles, hearing God's Word preached—I just loved it. This was what I had been seeking! During those weeks following the Akron meetings, George watched me closely. I knew he could see the change in me.

We were both members of the Greek Orthodox Church. The children and I attended many Sundays, but George would only attend on the High Holy Days. Still, I was praying constantly that George would offer to take me to the Kathryn Kuhlman services in Youngstown.

Then one day George came into the kitchen where I was fixing breakfast and said, "I bet you would like me to take you over to Youngstown to hear your preacher lady." I could not answer. It was too marvelous. All I could do was take his hand and blink back the tears.

"Well, you are not much of a nightclub goer," he went on, "so we will take the kids and drive over Sunday." That was the first of many Sundays we would spend driving the sixty miles from Akron to Youngstown to attend the worship services in Stambaugh Auditorium. George could see it made me happy. And even though I knew he was taking me only to ease his own conscience, I hoped enough of it would rub off on him that he would change.

Something was happening inside George. It was very gradual, but he was becoming more and more dissatisfied with his kind of life—and more and more amazed at how God's power was manifested in Miss Kuhlman's services.

Six months passed and the night clubs continued to operate, the entertainers came and went, and George still thought money was the most important thing in life.

The last Saturday night in January, 1953, Artie Shaw closed at the club and George came home feeling especially weary. "The roads are a thick mass of ice. It will be impossible to go to Youngstown tomorrow morning," he said. That night I prayed, knowing that God could melt the ice if He wanted us to go. And He did—for a very special reason.

The auditorium was packed and we had to take separate seats. George was sitting two rows in front of me with Bill, our second son, on his lap. I had Gus (our oldest) and Pattie (who was only a year and a half) with me.

When the invitation was given, an unusually large number responded to the altar call. I could not understand why so many were going forward since I believed the altar call was only for atheists and those who had committed great sins.

Then Miss Kuhlman returned to the microphone and said, "This altar call is for those who have never been born again—for those who have never confessed with their mouth Jesus Christ and received Him as their personal Saviour. You may belong to a church. But if you have never accepted Him as your personal Saviour, then this call is for you."

I sat upright in my seat. Had I heard correctly? "Oh *Theoma*, I did not know I had to receive Jesus as my Saviour. I am going to do it right now," I said. So I took Gus and Pattie and we started down the aisle. When we came to where George was sitting, I gently touched him and said, "Honey, let's go and receive Christ."

"Not this time," he said, shaking his head and looking straight ahead. "You go on if you want."

They ushered us to the platform and we knelt far back in one corner. Gus and little Pattie looked at me strangely and I whispered, "Miss Kuhlman is praying for people on the other side of the platform. Now is the time to ask God to forgive our sins." I bowed my head and began to pray, sincerely listing all the sins I could think of and asking God to forgive me. "Oh, my God," I prayed, "if I have forgotten anything, please remind me. I want it all forgiven."

Suddenly, I heard a man's voice praying. I had never heard such a sincere, beautiful voice. And his words! He was asking God to forgive all the things I had forgotten. I was afraid to look up, but finally forced myself to open my eyes. His suit was a shining silver gray and his face—it looked like the face of *Christos*. He seemed very tall.

Suddenly, all the Scriptures I had underlined in my Bible came flashing through my mind. There was the sound of wind. It was getting louder and louder. Turning to Gus I whispered, "Do you hear the wind?"

"No, Mom," he said, staring at me.

"Listen carefully. I can hear it. Look with me to see if any windows are open."

Little Gus moved close to me. "No, Mom, there is no wind and no window open."

Then the power of God fell over me. I began to sway. I tried to hold still but had absolutely no control of my body. Then I heard Miss Kuhlman saying, "That is real!" And she came quickly toward me, saying, "This is God."

She came close to me and put her hands gently on my head and began to pray. It was peace—glorious peace. All the voices faded away and I heard only the sound of the wind and saw the name of Jesus before my face, appearing as a ladder all the way to heaven—Jesus—Jesus—Jesus—Jesus.

After the service, I met George at his seat. I could see that he was confused and afraid. He did not want to talk about it; reality had always scared George. "Yes," he said, "I could see you had some kind of experience. That's okay, but it's not for me. Carol, I am not going to be a hypocrite. I have been born once and just don't see the need to be born again. It's just as simple as that."

I had been right about one thing. It was impossible for George to attend the meetings and hear the Gospel and remain the same. He was examining his life in a way he had never examined it before, and was slowly realizing that he lived in a world of make-believe.

During the next two years, he often mentioned the hell he had created for himself and for us. "What's the use of making money and losing your family and soul?" he mumbled one night. But I kept sending prayer requests into Miss Kuhlman's office and waiting for the time when the Holy Spirit would break through into his life.

Then one afternoon in 1955, he came home early. "I'm sick of it," he said, groping for the right words.

"What do you mean?" I asked.

"I mean I'm sick of myself and sick of the life I have gotten myself into. And Carol," he said, putting both hands on my shoulders, "if you will have me, I am going to be the best husband and father in the world."

His eyes were sincere, moist with tears, as he continued. "I'm going to sell the clubs. It is just not worth it to lose all that is precious just to make another buck. I am through with liquor and all that goes with it. I am going to be a different man." And George became a different man. He still had a long way to go before he made his total surrender to Christ, but he was on the way!

An old friend learned George had sold his clubs and offered him a job as a restaurant manager. It was a big cut in pay and we had to radically change our standard of living, but George said it was worth it to go to bed at night feeling clean inside.

Things were not easy. His old acquaintances were always coming in the restaurant and offering him drinks. "Come on, George," they would tempt him, "have a drink with your buddies." But George never gave an inch. Eventually his old buddies realized he was sincere and stopped tempting him.

The children and I kept praying for George to make his final commitment. Even though he had made such a radical change, I knew his life was still empty. He had cleaned up his life, but that was not enough. He had to let Jesus Christ come into his life and take full control.

My arthritis was getting worse and I kept remembering the doctor's wife in the wheelchair and knew I could soon be like her. The calcium deposits in the joints were extremely painful and the only relief seemed to come from hot compresses and heating pads.

It was in August, 1957, a blessed day for us, far more blessed than we realized at the time. We were on our way to the service in Youngstown when George asked, "How does it happen?"

"What do you mean?"

"How do people get healed?" he said.

"I don't know, I guess it is just the grace and mercy of God." Little did I know that the answer was less than an hour away.

We arrived at 10:45 A.M., but the auditorium was already packed. The only place we could find to stand was far back under the balcony. Miss Kuhlman was praying for the sick and we heard her say, "Someone is receiving a healing for the spine." She kept repeating it. Then she walked off the platform and pointed to the center section of the auditorium and said, "The Spirit bears witness—the healing is across the shoulders."

I turned to George and whispered, "Oh, I wish I could have that healing."

He turned and said, "Then why don't you ask the Lord for it?"

I could not believe it. George was giving me spiritual advice. "Of course!" I gasped. "What is the matter with me?" Lifting my hand upward, I quietly said, "Lord, I will take that healing."

With my eyes shut, I saw the Spirit of God as a pure white rod moving slowly, high across the audience from the stage toward the balcony. We were standing under the balcony and I saw it disappear over the top of the overhang. I continued to stand with my hand outstretched, ready to receive anything God gave me. And then, when it was directly over me, I suddenly felt a great overwhelming joy bursting in my heart. I wanted to shout; I wanted to sing. I was instantly aware that I had been healed of the curvature of the spine and the dreadful rheumatoid arthritis. "Praise the Lord!" I kept repeating over and over.

George pulled me close to him. "Something wonderful has happened to you, Carol."

On the way home I found I was able to close my fingers into a fist, something I had not been able to do in years. The pain was gone from my back and shoulders. There was no denying the power of God.

Two weeks later, we were able to return to Youngstown. When Miss Kuhlman gave the invitation for those who would accept Christ, I looked at George. His face was twisted in agony and torture as the contending forces in his life battled for the victory. I bowed my head in prayer, "Oh, *Theoma*, give him the victory."

When I lifted my head, he was not in his seat. Then I saw him. He was on the platform, kneeling in humble repentance receiving the Lord Jesus Christ as his personal Saviour. There were no vain promises, there was no bargaining with God, there was nothing hypocritical; he was simply surrendering everything he had to Jesus Christ.

George had come home.

14

A Clown Laughs Again

By Sanford Silsby

*Sandy Silsby is a teacher with the Escondido
Union School in Escondido, California. He works ex-
clusively with the More Able Learners (MAL)
group—children with especially high IQs. He is a native of Michigan and holds an A.B. degree from Eastern Michigan University and an M.A. from the
University of Michigan. His wife Margie is a nurse
and they have three children.*

This story is not about me—at least not directly.
Rather, I want to tell you about a friend of mine named
Virgil (Tiny) Poor. It would be best for Tiny to write his
own story, but he is not too good with words. So, Tiny
has asked me to tell you about it, just the way it happened.

In his better days, Tiny Poor had been a clown with
the MGM Studios. But during the last twenty years, he
had moved from one place to another, wandering all
over the West looking for some way out of his misery.

I first met him through my wife Margie who was a nurse at the local hospital. She told me about this poor man who was dragging his pain-wracked body up to that hospital trying to get help. He had been the custodian at the La Costa Downs Country Club in San Diego. He had the title of Assistant Building Engineer. "But," he always said with a grin, "I was just the janitor."

One evening in 1964, Tiny was coming down a flight of concrete steps outside the club house carrying a huge garbage can on his shoulder. It was dark and he misjudged a step and plunged fifteen feet down the stairs. He landed on his back and neck against a brick banister. He tried to work the next couple of days, but finally quit as the pain in his body grew worse and worse.

Tiny simply resigned himself to the pain. He did think it strange when other symptoms began to appear and he noticed painful swellings in all of his joints—knees, back, hips, knuckles, wrists. He finally went to a doctor who diagnosed his condition as arthritis and loaded him down with pills—pain-killing pills.

He was now lonely and alone, unable to support himself even though he was in his early fifties. The knuckles on both hands were swollen out of shape. He could turn his neck only about fifteen degrees in either direction. His back was so filled with arthritis that it was only with teeth-gritting determination that he could sit down and getting up was pure torture. His hips, knees, and lower spine were becoming so calcified that even walking was a painful experience.

The doctors could take X-rays and give him pills, but they could not cure him. This type of arthritis is incurable and progressive. It cannot be halted in its ruthless advance that finally leaves its victim crippled and bedridden.

I had grown to love Tiny as a lonely and forsaken man who lived in a tenant house on an old ranch outside Escondido. One evening after school, I drove out and found him sitting in his living room in the dark. His face was wet from tears.

"This afternoon, I tried to weed my garden," he said. "I pulled two weeds, but the pain was so bad I could not stand it. I cried like a baby and I think if I had a gun, I might have killed myself."

My heart went out to Tiny, but I felt helpless to do anything for him. The Welfare Department had sent him to Los Angeles to be examined by the State Disability Board and they had declared him totally disabled. He was drawing a small pension, but a few paltry dollars were small compensation for the pain and the prospect of ultimate incapacitation.

"Only God can help Tiny," I said to Margie when I returned home that night. I believed in God and I had always had a strong faith that He was opposed to suffering, disease, and human misery. But I was not much of a church goer and I knew I lacked spiritual power in my life. How could I encourage Tiny with spiritual help when I had no power myself?

A short time later, Margie's brother Frank Hines, a Chicago lawyer, sent her a copy of John Sherrill's book *They Speak With Other Tongues.* She read it and then began to urge me to read it also. For the first time, I saw in words what I had seemed to know existed all along—the power of God manifested by the Holy Spirit.

I did not realize it at the time, but God was manipulating the time schedule of my life and Tiny's life also. The day I finished the book, I received a letter from Frank. In the letter, he shared a powerful testimony of the transformation that Jesus had made in his life as a result of this same source of power: the Holy Spirit. The book and the letter provoked me to hunger for this same power. I began to search for others who shared the same feeling.

All this time, I was praying for Tiny. I guess I felt that if I could find the answers to my own spiritual quest, I could share them with him. He had accepted Christ as his personal Saviour and when I suggested we ought to try spiritual healing for his body, he agreed. I promised him that I would begin a search for someone who had been given the Christian gift of healing and could minister to Tiny through the Holy Spirit.

Thus, compelled by my own desire to receive the power of the Holy Spirit and prompted by my longing to help Tiny with his physical needs, I attended a meeting of the Full Gospel Businessmen's Fellowship in Oceanside. I asked the first man I met if he knew of any Christian who had been given the gift of healing.

"It must have been the Holy Spirit that sent you to me," he replied. "I am an usher at the Kathryn Kuhlman meetings in Los Angeles. She does not claim to be a healer, but miracles take place when she conducts a service." I told him of Tiny's condition and he promised to meet him at the stage entrance of the Shrine Auditorium at the next service and help him find a seat before the service began.

In looking back, it seems like another minor miracle in a long chain of miracles that God had guided directly to this usher. It would have been impossible for Tiny to have waited outside since he could only stand for short periods of time. I told Tiny and we made arrangements to attend the service in April 1967.

I read Kathryn Kuhlman's book, *I Believe in Miracles,* telling about countless sufferers who had been healed through the power of the Holy Spirit. I read the chapter on arthritis to Tiny. Tears came to his eyes and he asked, "Do you think it could happen to me?" I found myself praying daily for Tiny's healing and asking others to pray.

The Sunday finally arrived when Kathryn Kuhlman would be in Los Angeles. Margie could not go, but she packed us a tasty lunch. I took my two sons, Charles and Ford, and we drove out and picked up Tiny from his humble cottage on the ranch and began the long drive up the coast to Los Angeles.

We were so anxious to attend the service that we arrived an hour earlier than we had planned. I took Tiny to the stage entrance and we talked to the doorman. Yes, he knew our usher friend and suggested that Tiny take a seat just inside the door on an old-fashioned, wooden folding chair. He would point him out to the usher so he could find him a seat in the auditorium.

Confident that all was well, the boys and I went around to the front of the auditorium. More than a thousand people had already arrived although it was only 11:45 A.M. and the doors did not open until 1:00 P.M. All three of us felt that this was Tiny's day. God was surely going to heal him.

The service was marvelous. After the song service, Miss Kuhlman's first statement was, "Medical science says that arthritis is incurable. At these services, many people have been healed of arthritis by the Holy Spirit."

This is Tiny's day, I thought excitedly. "Oh, hurry, God, hurry and heal him," I prayed. I did not know where Tiny was sitting, but knew he was somewhere in that vast throng of people, waiting expectantly for the power to fall on him.

Then we got caught up in the content of Miss Kuhlman's sermon. While she was preaching, I was aware that healings began to take place all around us. The Spirit of God was sweeping through that great auditorium touching people's bodies. Shortly thereafter, they began to come to the stage asking if they could testify about the miracle.

The very first person to come to the microphone was a lady who had been healed of arthritis. She bent over and touched the floor—something she said she had not been able to do for years. My heart was in my throat as I stretched my neck looking for Tiny. I expected him on the platform any moment.

Then the testimonies began to come so fast that I was almost off my feet from the impact. A six-year-old boy had been healed of curvature of the spine. His mother was with him, weeping for joy. A lady dressed in furs came up holding two hearing aids in her hand. She was from a church in Beverly Hills. A man came carrying a leg brace. We sat spellbound at the wonderful things God was doing.

An elderly lady came up in a wheelchair. She kept repeating over and over, "I have been healed."

"Well, then, get up and walk," Miss Kuhlman said.

Stiffly and with the greatest effort, she pulled herself upright from the wheelchair. At first her knees were partially bent and her back stooped, but she hobbled across the stage. Gradually, her knees and back straightened and she was walking back and forth, chuckling to herself, tears running down her face as she praised God. She ended up giving others rides across the stage in her own wheelchair.

There were many, many other healings. Some of the people around me who had been healed were too excited to go to the stage. Some others may not have recognized that they had been healed. It was a grand sight.

I had read all about the miracles of God in the Bible. I had heard ministers talk of the power of God from their pulpits. But this was the first time I had ever really seen God's power with my own eyes. But where was Tiny? What had happened to him? The boys kept looking out over the audience trying to spot him, but we never could see him. The benediction was pronounced and the people were leaving. Tiny had disappeared.

We found the usher, but he hadn't seen Tiny at all. We all began looking for him, but he was not to be found. We finally went to the car and waited. Forty-five minutes passed and the sidewalks around the auditorium were almost deserted. Tiny still had not shown up. By now we were genuinely worried.

I went back to the stage entrance where we had left him. The door was ajar and the inside room was dark. I peeked in and there was Tiny—sitting on that same wooden folding chair where we had left him. As he came out, he shook his head and said, "This is the darnedest place."

Gradually, the story unfolded. Shortly after we left him, the doorman was changed. The new doorman did not know the usher or that Tiny was waiting for him. The usher, who had never met Tiny, arrived and looked for me. When he could not see me, he thought we had taken Tiny in some other way and left to take up his ushering duties. And Tiny had sat on that wooden folding chair from 11 A.M. until 5:30 P.M., waiting for someone to tell him what to do.

He never heard a thing that went on in the auditorium, nor did he ever see Miss Kuhlman. He had sat on that hard chair for six and a half hours.

I was confused, disappointed, and angry. We had been so excited about the service that we had not double-checked to see that Tiny had gotten in; yet, our primary purpose in coming was to bring Tiny. At first, I blamed myself. Then I was angry at the usher. Then, in my frustration, I did not know who to blame.

Tiny said very little as we drove home. The boys and I were bubbling over with the excitement of what we had seen and heard. Yet we hesitated talking about it because Tiny was right there and had missed the whole thing. We tried to explain what had gone on in the services, but since he had missed it all, he could not visualize the wonderful things that had transpired.

I apologized to Tiny again as I dropped him off at his house. We made tentative plans to go again with better arrangements.

Margie was just as bewildered as I when she learned what had happened. I went to school the next morning, but even my normally exciting job working with the special children was depressing. In fact, I was so downcast I could hardly wait for the day to end. After dinner, Margie and I decided to go out and see Tiny to try to cheer him up. "If I am this discouraged," I said, "think how he must feel."

We turned off the highway and drove the long road into the old ranch. In the distance, we could see Tiny's little cottage. The front door was open when we drove up and through the screen we could see Tiny sitting in the living room.

Margie and I tried to offer our feeble excuses for what had gone wrong, but after awhile we gave up and gave Tiny a chance to talk. It finally occurred to me that he had spoken but a few words since 5:30 P.M. the day before.

"Guess what I have been doing?" he said. "I've been weeding in the garden all afternoon. Look, look!" He got up from his chair, bent over, touched the floor and cried out, "I've been healed. I've been healed."

I could hardly believe my eyes. Even the swellings on his knuckles had disappeared. "But when, Tiny? When did it happen?" I cried.

"Why, it happened yesterday at the Shrine."

"Yesterday? But you didn't even get in the auditorium," I objected.

"I know," he said. "It happened while I was sitting out there on that chair."

"But why didn't you say something about it on the way home?" I asked in frustration.

"I was afraid it wasn't real. I was afraid it would go away. But this morning when I got up, it was just like I had springs in my legs. I went out and pulled the weeds out of the garden and I have worked hard all day. It's the first time I have been able to do any work in a year and a half."

"Tiny," Margie said, "tell us what happened."

"Well," he said, grinning and scratching the back of his neck. "Sandy and them left me on that chair in the hallway outside the auditorium. I never got up. I wanted to get up once and go to the bathroom, but was afraid if I did that the usher who was supposed to come after me would miss me. Every time I saw a man coming in my direction, I would think it was the usher. But no one ever came after me."

He paused, trying to remember the exact details. "I knew the service was going on inside the building, but I never heard anything, never saw the stage, didn't even know what was going on. I just sat there. Then, about 4:30 P.M., I felt a huge electric shock shaking my body.

It made me tingle and burn inside." He grinned, embarrassed, and continued, "It was the same feeling I used to have when I would take a big drink of raw whisky and feel it hit my bloodstream. Only this time there was no hangover—just joy and peace.

"I looked at my hands. 'My gosh, I can move them,' I said out loud. I sat there, wiggling my fingers. I tried to move my knees. I had been sitting so long in that one place that everything about me had gotten stiff. But I finally got up and walked about twenty feet to one side and everything worked perfectly—just like it did when I was a clown back at MGM twenty years ago."

Tiny shrugged his shoulders and grinned widely. "Then about 5:30, Sandy came back for me. I didn't understand what was going on. I knew something had happened to me, but I was afraid to say very much right then. I guess it was God after all."

Margie and I returned home with singing hearts. Everybody else had forgotten about Tiny—everybody but God. And God had overcome man's obstructions and had beamed His healing power right into the heart of a lonely, forgotten man. And Tiny Poor has never been the same since.

I said at the beginning that this story was about Tiny and it is. But I cannot help but mention that my life has been changed, too. Every time I go back to the Shrine Auditorium, I grin and say, "You know, this is the darnedest place!"

15

Be Careful How You Pray
by Freda Longstaff

*So remarkable was the healing of Freda Longstaff
that United Press International (UPI) published the
facts regarding the miracle. I did not meet Freda until after she had been healed because the lengthening
of her leg took place in the bedroom of her own home
and not in a miracle service. No one can tell it better
than Freda herself.*

"Dear Jesus, please help Bill. We need him so much
and he is in so much pain. Please, Jesus, I will not ask
you to heal me now if you will just heal Bill."

It was the first real prayer I had ever prayed. But we
were at the end of our rope. Bill, my husband, had been
injured in England in 1945, seven years before. He had
been a chief radio operator during the war and, during
an air raid in Ramsbury, had been knocked down a flight
of steps and hurt his back. He did not report it since there
was such a critical shortage of men in his outfit, but after the war it got much worse. Now it was very bad.

The doctor said he could do nothing except keep him strapped and braced.

The time was fast approaching when he would be confined to a wheelchair for the rest of his life. The only relief Bill seemed to get was through constant chiropractic adjustments. Bill was a big man, but sometimes he would cry when he walked, the pain was so intense.

Neither of us was very religious. Bill had grown up in the Church of God in Anderson, Indiana, and I had been a Methodist all my life. But recently we had been desperately searching for something real in our spiritual lives. The hunger—oh, the spiritual hunger we felt. And it was more intense because of Bill's suffering.

I, too, was deformed—actually far more deformed than Bill. I had been born with a congenital dislocation of both hips and a curvature of the spine. I was seven years old when my folks took me to the Children's Hospital in Columbus, Ohio, and the doctors had performed corrective bone surgery on both hips. "She will walk," they told my parents, "but she will always be deformed."

They were right. My left hip stuck way out on one side, and because of its dislocation, my left knee turned inward and threw my leg out in an awkward manner each time I took a step. But I had been able to have two children, although my doctor had said I must not have any more.

I was not concerned about my own physical deformities. I was concerned about Bill.

It was a cold, rainy morning. I was wakened by the ringing phone and heard Bill talking to his mother and father. They wanted us to ride over to Pittsburgh with them. Bill shouted up the steps to see if I wanted to go. "If Audrey will keep the children, it is all right with me,"

I said. In very short order, we were out on the highway heading toward Pittsburgh which was sixty miles away.

All Bill's mother and father could talk about were the Kathryn Kuhlman miracle services in Pittsburgh. I looked at Bill out of the corner of my eye. He asked, "Is this where we are going?"

"Your father has been after me to go to one of the services," Bill's mother said innocently, "so we thought you would like to come along."

Bill glanced out the window at the steady drizzle of rain. "Come on, Dad...," Bill began, but I poked him with my elbow. We had come too far now to turn around and I could see that his parents had their hearts set on us going with them.

It was a miserable day. Bill's dad insisted on going directly to Carnegie Hall although the doors were not scheduled to open until five o'clock in the evening and we had arrived at eight o'clock in the morning. "Dad, for goodness sake, are we going to have to wait here all day?" Bill complained.

But his dad was stubborn and would have it no other way. "If we don't arrive early, we don't get a good seat."

"I know, but nine hours early?" Bill asked.

It was the longest wait I had ever endured. The rain was drizzling and everyone had raincoats and umbrellas. But since I was so much shorter than everyone else, it seemed that all the rain was dripping off the umbrellas and down the back of my neck. My hips hurt and my legs were killing me. I thought of poor Bill. He sat on the wide, concrete banisters for awhile, but they were cold and wet, so he leaned disgustedly against the wall.

Some of Bill's dad's friends, Catholics from Warwood, had joined us and were chatting away, oblivious to the horrible weather. The rain turned to sleet and I was miserable and uncomfortable.

By noon, the press of the crowd was so great that we could not have left if we wanted to. We were pushed almost flat against the front doors. Being first may have its advantages, unless you are the first one into the bottom of a barrel. I was so miserable!

When the doors finally opened, we were swept into the vestibule with the crowd. There was no hesitating, no turning, no holding back, or else we would have been crushed in the mob of pushing, shoving people. We wanted to sit on the main floor, but the part of the crowd we were in somehow turned and headed toward the right balcony. We had no choice but to go along or be trampled. Bill's dad and one of his friends grabbed Bill by the elbows and literally carried him up the stairs to keep him from being crushed. It was incredible.

The service started a few minutes before six. Immediately, things began to happen—not to us, but around us. Bill could not seem to take his eyes off a little woman sitting several seats down on our right who was shaking violently. I kept punching him, trying to get him to pay attention to Miss Kuhlman. But every time I looked up at him, he was staring at that poor little woman who was trying so hard to control her violent trembling.

"What is wrong with her?" Bill whispered loudly. Too loudly, for everyone in our section turned and looked at us. I was afraid to look at her.

Then Miss Kuhlman called out that someone was being healed of a curvature of the spine and this woman got up and went downstairs.

"Did you see that?" Bill said in a loud voice. "All that shaking, and now she is healed. Look at her. There she goes up on the stage." More people were looking at

Bill than were watching the little woman. But he just sat there, his eyes as big as saucers.

"Shhh," I said to Bill, trying to calm him down. He just looked at me and shook his head in dismay. "I cannot believe it," he muttered.

The one thing that impressed me more than anything else was a statement Miss Kuhlman made. It was as though she were speaking directly to me. "Nothing is impossible with God." It followed me home that day and stayed with me. "Nothing is impossible with God."

At that time, we lived in a duplex apartment next to Bill's sister and brother-in-law, Audrey and Sherl Tyler, in Warwood, West Virginia. The following Tuesday, Bill and his brother-in-law decided to drive back into Pittsburgh to another service, a preaching service. When they got home at eleven o'clock that night, Audrey and I were waiting up for them.

They were too excited to eat supper. Both had made extensive notes and had their pockets stuffed with folded papers. Bill said, "Honey, this is what we have been looking for all along. I know it. This is the answer to our search." And it was the answer.

Bill and Sherl were so excited about the teaching of the Bible that Miss Kuhlman had given in the service that they were both trying to talk at the same time. They repeated word for word everything that she had said. It was all so new to us, so thrilling, for we had never had the Bible explained to us like that. We sat up for hours that night, reading the Bible and looking up the Scriptures that Miss Kuhlman had read during the service. My heart seemed to beat a little faster and Bill was more excited than I had ever seen him in all our married life. Suddenly God had become real to us and it was as though His presence were right there in the room. There was no sleep in any of us. No one wanted to sleep. We were not hungry nor were we tired. We had found something we had been searching for all our lives.

It was two o'clock in the morning when Audrey and Sherl reluctantly left. I climbed the stairs in our little duplex apartment to my bedroom. The only way Bill could climb the stairs was on his knees and elbows, so he slept downstairs on the dining room table in a crazy, bent position to relieve some of the pain in his back. Many times he spent the night sitting up in a chair with a pillow on his lap, bent over in an awkward position to ease the pain.

Reaching my bedroom, I fell on my twisted knees and began to pray. Suddenly, something began to happen there at the bedside. It was as though a tent of some kind had been lowered around me and covered me completely. I was entirely shut off from the outside world. I felt myself begin to rise. I stopped praying, having a strange sensation that it was not necessary anymore. There were no more words as I felt myself being drawn up to some great unknown height. It was a slow, lifting process as though I were in an open elevator. I was aware of nothing but the rising sensation.

Then, just as I seemed to reach some kind of a summit, I felt a strange, tingling sensation in my hips—then a grinding noise. It was the bones in my hips. I could feel them moving, grating together. I was powerless to control it, but even on my knees I could feel my body moving and shifting as a powerful, yet so gentle, force put it into perfect alignment. Then my knees, as I felt them being pulled back into their proper position, scraped inward across the floor until they were lined up with my hips.

I was scared, afraid to move. I knew I was being healed, but I was afraid to speak a word. The tears began to flow. I made no sound, just continued to kneel and weep silently.

I have no idea how long the whole process took. It seemed like ages, but I suspect it was over in just a few moments. But then the bones finally stopped moving and I felt another sensation going through my body. It was much like I had stuck my finger in an electric socket and the current was flowing through me from the top of my head to the soles of my feet. I could feel my body vibrating from the current. Then it, too, faded.

I felt myself being lowered slowly, coming down, just as I had been lifted up. When I reached the "bottom," the covering was slowly removed and I was once again aware of my surroundings. I looked across the bed at the mirror on the dresser. How different I looked! Then I said out loud, "I have been healed, I have been healed."

"Bill," I called out, "you have to come up here right away!" I could hear him rousing.

"What is it, Freda?" he mumbled.

"I can't tell you," I was almost crying, "but please hurry."

I could hear him crawling up the steps. I knew how painful and difficult it was for him. He finally reached the top and I heard him groan in pain as he got to his feet. He came to the door and peered in. "What is it, Freda? Are you all right?"

My voice was shaking as I looked up from my kneeling position. Bill stood framed in the doorway. "Bill, I've been healed."

He tried to move toward me, but seemed to be stopped dead in his tracks by some invisible force. He made another move toward me but fell back into the door.

"Bill, please call Audrey and Sherl. Something has happened to me. I have been healed."

Bill backed out of the room and I heard him moving as quickly as he could through the children's bedroom to the connecting upstairs door to the Tyler's apartment. He pounded on the door as he called out, "Freda says she's been healed. You all get over here as fast as you can."

Bill came back and began pulling at my arm, trying to get me off my knees. "No, Bill, I am afraid to stand up. But I know God touched me. I felt it."

Audrey burst into the room in her pajamas and fell to her knees beside my bed. Moments later, Sherl knelt beside her and then Bill, groaning from the pain, clumsily knelt beside me.

None of us were Christians, but we all tried to pray anyway. I remember Audrey praying, "Dear God, please forgive my sins." And I thought, yes, that's what I ought to say, too. And I did. And as I did, I felt the same sensation of electric-like current running through my body again. He has answered my prayer, I thought, I have been saved. But I didn't know how to say it or what to do about it.

Bill pulled himself to his feet and tried to pull me up. At last, I was able to get my legs under me and slowly stood. I ran my hands down the sides of my hips and down my legs where the awful deformities had been moments before. They were perfectly straight. I moved toward the door and before I knew it, I was running down the steps, into the living room, through the kitchen, back through the dining area where Bill's pillow and cover were still on the table.   I was running...laughing and running.

I heard Bill and then Sherl on the telephone. It was not long before there was a pounding on the front door and in came my parents, then Bill's, then Sherl's. All joined in the strange rejoicing as I pranced back and forth like a fashion model in front of a house full of astonished people. And at 3 A.M., we had the wildest pajama party ever to hit Warwood.

The next week Bill and Sherl went back to Pittsburgh. I do not think wild horses could have kept them away. When they returned to Warwood, we had a prayer meeting in Audrey's living room in the middle of the night.

Bill had reached a stage of desperation. God had obviously healed me when I wasn't even asking for it. Now Bill wanted a healing for himself. I had never seen him the way he was that night, literally challenging God to do something.

Even though I knew nothing about praying, I shuddered when it came his turn to pray. He was not thanking God like the rest of us, he was almost shouting at Him. "God, why is it that all these others seem to know You and I do not know You. You healed Freda—why don't You heal me? You have just got to prove yourself to me!" Bill almost hollered these last words.

Suddenly, it was as though some unseen giant hand had picked him up and he was literally thrown against the door frame. Bill weighed almost two hundred pounds at the time, but this force effortlessly tossed him across the room. He lay in an almost lifeless heap, piled against the door frame.

I remember screaming and Sherl and Audrey looked at him with wide-eyed terror. All we knew was we had heard Bill pray this awful prayer and then he was slammed against the wall hard enough to break his body into pieces.

Bill's eyes were still wide open and he began shouting again. "God, I am desperate! I challenge You! Do something for me!" Again, that great unseen force knocked him down onto the floor. It was as though he had been struck by lightning!

Suddenly Sherl said, "Maybe it's because he hasn't eaten. That's why he can't stand up."

I knew good and well that the lack of food wasn't knocking Bill across the room, but I thought perhaps it would be a good idea to try to get some nourishment into him. So the three of us tried to pull him to his feet. But he was too heavy to move. His body seemed lifeless, without movement. We were frightened and I began to plead with him to get up. "Please, Bill, try."

His lips moved and he mumbled, "I cannot move. I cannot do anything for myself." Still, we managed to get him into a chair in the kitchen.

While we were rushing around, frying bacon and eggs, I saw Bill suddenly straighten up in the chair and then, as though that same giant hand had slapped him across the back, he skidded across the kitchen floor and crashed heavily into the refrigerator. We just stood there in stark unbelief.

Softly, tenderly, I heard him begin to praise the Lord, worshiping Jesus and thanking Him for His goodness. He was praying the penitent's prayer, asking forgiveness as a little child would ask the forgiveness of a parent.

I bent over his prone body. And sure enough, I could actually hear the bones in his back snapping and cracking. I knew that Bill was being healed.

Moments later, he stood to his feet, supporting himself with one hand on the refrigerator. He stood erect in the middle of the floor and a slow grin spread over his face. "Wow!" he said softly, shaking his head. "Whatever that was, it fixed my back. The pain is gone. Look!" He began to bend and twist, touching the floor with his fingertips. That night, for the first time in months and months, he was able to stretch out on his bed and sleep without pain.

The rest is history.

A Catholic friend notified the local paper, *The Wheeling News Register*, and the reporters came out and took our picture and ran it on the front page. The United Press International picked it up and it was carried nationwide on the wire service. Our hearts were so filled with joy and gladness that we told God we would follow His leading into any field He desired, and that we would follow Him unconditionally. Bill was ordained as a minister and was asked to be a pastor of a small church. We accepted and have been in this phase of the ministry ever since.

My doctor had warned me not ever to have any more children. "Your hips and pelvis cannot stand it," he had said. But a year later, I gave birth to a little girl. There were no complications and I went through childbirth with flying colors. And then, as though to add frosting on the cake, God allowed me to give birth to twin boys seven years later. When my former doctor learned of this, he just threw up his hands and said, "Physically impossible!"

Bill and I just grinned; we knew better!

16

Cold Turkey
by Nick Cadena

Nick Cadena is literally a miracle of this century. Today, I am so proud of him, for he is one of the reasons why I gladly give my life as a living sacrifice to preach the Gospel.

Nick, thirty-six years old, works in a machine shop in Los Angeles. He is married and the father of three girls. He was first arrested at the age of nine and spent the majority of the next fifteen years in jail. By the time he was eighteen, he was addicted to heroin, a habit which continued for fifteen years and cost him up to a hundred dollars a day before he kicked it cold turkey (without the use of drugs or medication during withdrawal).

There is nothing pretty about a junkie. Dope addiction ravages the mind and body and turns a person into an animal—a sick, shaking, vomiting, stealing animal.

The gang I ran around with as a nine-year-old kid was made up of older boys. My parents knew little about my associates until it was too late to do anything about it. Most of the kids in my crowd were taking pills, drinking, smoking pot, and sniffing glue. Just a few days before my tenth birthday, I was picked up by the cops along with some of the others. From then on, I was in jail more than I was out.

As I graduated from one crime category to another, so I climbed the ladder of stimulants and narcotics. Pep pills and their multi-colored depressant cousins led me to marijuana, which became a springboard to heroin.

My friends told me I would get more of a kick out heroin than the dissatisfying milder drugs. The pep pills and depressants always left you with a let down feeling. Marijuana was the same way. I had developed a tremendous craving for something more powerful. Heroin, I was told, was the ultimate.

I had been sentenced to three years in Juvenile Hall, Lancaster Prison, for possession of a .45 caliber pistol that had been used in a holdup. When I was paroled at the age of eighteen, I sought out a pusher and took my first shot of heroin. I was addicted.

If only I could have seen the future that stretched out before me like an endless horror movie. Little did I know that I would spend lonely, torturous hours in jail while my guts climbed the bars of my rib cage, screaming for a release that could be found only by doing dope. Little did I know I would be begging, stealing, robbing, even stealing from my own children to get enough money to buy my next shot. If there is such a thing as hell on earth, then it is found in the world of the junkie.

My last four years as an addict cost me up to a hundred dollars a day to keep me supplied. I had to steal almost five times that amount to support my habit since a "fence" will only give twenty percent on the dollar for stolen goods. This means that, conservatively speaking, during the last four years of my addiction, I stole close to half a million dollars to keep my habit supplied.

I got it any place I could. I stole from apartments, sometimes cleaning out all the furniture and clothing. I shoplifted, broke into stores and into delivery trucks, almost anywhere, so I could just get my hands on enough money for the next shot.

I could not count the times Pauline and my three little girls waited through the long, endless hours, sometimes days, for me to come home. There is little room or need for a wife in the tortured existence of the dope addict. Normal desires for success, achievement, physical pleasures, even sex and food, are deadened by the drug. When the addict emerges from his brief periods of artificial bliss to face the agonizing truth, his only escape is to deaden the shame with another shot. And so the endless circle continues, getting worse all the time.

One night I found myself aboard a city bus. I do not know how I got there. I came to on the back seat and was aware that I was sitting on something uncomfortable. I felt under my hip and discovered a small black book. When I staggered off the bus and to my apartment I took it with me. I later discovered that the black book was the Holy Bible. I had no intention of reading it, but something made me drop it into the dresser drawer. Little did I know that six months later I would turn to that little black book to find a release from my bondage.

I was becoming desperate. From the moment I awakened until my anxiety-ridden body fell into a stupor, perhaps two or three days later, I was totally occupied with ways and means of satisfying my insatiable craving for the drug. I moved with a frightening singleness of purpose toward that one moment when the prick of the nee-

dle signaled release from all the problems I couldn't handle. For an hour or so I would nod in my pleasant eu-
phoria, then the symptoms would begin to return and I
would have to think about getting more money to buy
another bag of the white powder. The cycle was continual, relentless. There seemed to be no hope, ever, of escape.

On a bright Sunday morning in March 1965, I left the
house to find Campbell, my pusher, a fellow junkie about
my age. Normally, the relationship between a junkie and
his pusher is the brief, secretive encounter of buyer and
seller in a transaction involving the little cellophane bag.
But I had known Campbell for a long time and we had
developed a friendship.

I was staggering down the street, sick, vomiting, and
crying in my heart for help. I had to stop several times
and lean against the side of the building, retching until
the spasms passed and I could stagger on. All the people seemed happy—all except me.

I met Campbell at his house. "Hey, Nick," he said,
"you know what? There's gonna be a lady at Angelus
Temple who is going to tell about God. I've been to her
services before. I believe she can set us free. Man, it'll
cost me because you're my best customer. But Nick,
you're gonna die if you stay like this. Let's go. Okay?
Maybe she'll pray for us both and we can kick the habit,
huh?"

I was in no mood for his crazy talk. I slapped my
money on the table and fell on top of it, reaching out to
grab hold of his shirt and shake the heroin out of him.
Campbell sensed my desperateness and quickly pro-
duced the powder and the "works," the stuff needed to
fix the shot.

With frantic fingers, I tore the top off the bag and shook the contents into a spoon. With a medicine dropper, which was part of the works Campbell supplied, I mixed a few drops of water with the powder. Campbell held a match under the spoon until the powder dissolved. I fashioned a quick tourniquet around my upper arm with my belt. The big vein in my elbow was clearly visible and, along with it, hundreds of little black dots from the countless number of fixes before.

As I had done many times in the past, I pushed the head of the hypodermic needle into the vein and then took the medicine dropper and filled it from the solution in the spoon. Slowly, very slowly, I dropped the clear liquid into the open end of the metal needle and squeezed the vein to get it into the blood system.

Immediately, I felt a wave of calm and peacefulness sweep over me. My shaking stopped and I leaned back and lighted a cigarette. For a long time, I sat nodding in the characteristic fashion of the addict who has found temporary relief.

"Hey, man," I finally said. "What was this you said about a lady preacher?"

"Yeah," Campbell said, "I've been to some of her meetings. She's great! I mean, guys get healed of all sorts of things. You gotta see it to believe it. I bet if she laid her hands on you, you'd kick the habit. You wanna go?"

I had tried everything else and nothing worked. And the desperateness was about to kill me. I was willing to try anything—even this.

And so that night Campbell and I found ourselves high in the balcony of the huge Angelus Temple in Los Angeles, California. I had never been to a church meeting in all my life. I had never even heard the Gospel. The room was jammed with people. I have never seen such a mob. Everyone was praising God. But the sermon, well, it was difficult for me to understand. As a matter of fact, I didn't even listen. The effect of the shot was beginning to wear off and I was starting to get that tense, anxious feeling that hits a junkie before he needs another fix.

Suddenly, Campbell was punching me with his elbow. "Hey, Nick, she's giving an altar call. Come on. Let's go down. She'll pray for you and put her hands on you and you'll be set free. Let's go." I shook my head, but he persisted and we finally made our way to the exit, down the stairs to the lobby, and started down the long aisle to the front of the auditorium.

About halfway down, I started back. Campbell grabbed my arm, "Hey, what's up, man? You can't go back now. Everyone's looking at you. You gotta go down." I reluctantly agreed, but was able to hide on the back edge of the huge crowd that had gathered around the front during the altar call.

Suddenly the crowd seemed to open up and I saw Miss Kuhlman staring down that alley of people—right at me. "You," she said, pointing her finger at me. "You, young man. You need Jesus. If you will just come here, I will be so glad to pray for you."

I glanced to both sides. She couldn't be talking about me. I didn't even know who she was or what I was doing there. But she kept pointing that long finger right at me. She was starting to walk toward me, beckoning me with that finger to step forward. I tried to turn and run, but more people had gathered behind me and there was no way out.

"I mean you, young man," she said again with an authoritative voice. "Come up here and I will pray for you."

I found myself walking down that canyon of people. She met me at the front edge of the crowd and laid her hands on my head and began to pray. Before I knew it, I was on the floor. I scrambled to my feet and gave her a frightened stare before bolting back through the crowd to where Campbell was still standing.

"Come on, man, let's get out of here. I can't take this. That woman bugs me. Man, I gotta have a fix." I was still staggering under the tremendous surge of power that had flowed through my body. But there was something else. I was afraid, more afraid than I had been in all my life.

We went to Campbell's house where I got a fix. It did not do the trick and I made him give me another one. "Nicky, you're liable to get an overdose," he said. "You'll die."

"I can't help it," I said, "something has happened to me and I have to get a fix so I can calm down."

That night, I had nightmares. Over and over, I woke up screaming. I remembered the Bible and staggered to my dresser and scrambled through the clothes until I found it. Pauline turned on the light and I sat on the edge of the bed and opened the book and began reading in the Book of Revelation. I understood nothing I read, but I read that entire book. Then Pauline and I spent the rest of the night talking. She sensed that something big had happened in my life, something frightening and awesome, but she was unable to cope with what it was.

"If anything happens to me, I am not ready," I said.

"Ready for what, Nick?" she said.

"I'm not ready to die," I gasped out, "and I think I'm about to die."

"How do you get ready to die?" she asked, her eyes brimming with tears.

"I don't know, I don't know, I don't know," I screamed and fell across the bed, pounding the mattress with my fist. "All I know is that I'm not ready." This went on for three months, until I thought I'd go crazy. I was spending a hundred dollars a day on heroin and eating only when Pauline forced something in me. I didn't know it then, but from the moment Miss Kuhlman laid her hands on me, the Holy Spirit had gone to work in my life. I realize now that He had been at work around me for a long time. He had placed the Bible. He had driven me to Campbell's house. He had influenced Campbell to take me to the service. But that night the Holy Spirit had entered my life and I was under what I now know was conviction of the sin in my life.

I was running, battling, fighting as hard as I could. Yet, like Saul on the road to Damascus, you can only struggle so long and then you have to knuckle under to God.

And so one evening, the first of the summer, I staggered up the steps of Teen Challenge in Los Angeles. I knew that these people were dedicated to helping dope addicts kick the habit. I didn't know their procedures. I didn't know anything about them. All I knew was I needed to kick the habit and people had said they would help me.

The moment I walked in the door, I felt the power of the Holy Spirit over me again, much like that night in Angelus Temple. And what had started that night in the Kathryn Kuhlman service, three months before, was completed at Teen Challenge as I kicked the habit—cold turkey.

I stayed at Teen Challenge two months, getting my feet on the ground, spiritually as well as physically. When I returned home, Pauline greeted a new man.

Since then, Pauline and all three of the girls have given their hearts to the Lord. A Christian businessman gave me a job in his machine shop. I had never had a job before because I didn't have time to work, I was so busy stealing. But my new boss realized it would take time for me to learn how to work and has been patient with me. He gives me time off to preach and witness to others about the wonderful grace of God. Recently, I have enrolled in Bible school to further my knowledge of God's Word.

The big thrill of my life is once a month when I attend the miracle services at the Shrine. At a recent meeting, I was on the stage when more than a hundred hippies responded to a special invitation. They poured from the balcony and trooped to the platform, committing their lives to Jesus. It was a stirring moment as the Holy Spirit swept through the great mass of people and touched lives and hearts. Boys with long, shaggy beards and hair falling past their shoulders, and girls, dressed in Indian costumes with floor-length dresses and hair past their waists, came and stood in a huge semicircle on the stage.

Miss Kuhlman moved briskly through the crowd laying on hands and praying. Many of the boys and girls collapsed under the power of God and then regained their feet, hugging each other in joy.

I noticed one girl in particular, certainly no older than thirteen, hugging a tiny, newborn baby to her breast. She was like all the others—barefooted, with long hair, and Indian garb. But her eyes were full of indescribable sadness as she clutched that tiny baby.

Then Miss Kuhlman called on me to lead them from the stage to a side room where we could talk and pray. As we marched off the platform, many of them were holding their fingers in the traditional "V" sign, which is popular among the flower children. Today, that sign has a new meaning, I thought to myself.

After the service a skeptical friend of mine just shook his head. "It will not last, Nick," he said. "Those kids do not have the slightest idea what they are doing. They just came because the rest of the crowd came. Sure they fell under the power, but it will wear off. Just you wait and see."

I did not argue with him. But I thought back to a little over three years before when the same thing happened to me. I had no idea why I came forward, either. I came only because someone forced me to. I fell under the power and had no knowledge of what had happened. I had no one to train me. I had no Sunday school to attend—no pastor to guide me. All I had was that copy of the Bible I had found on the bus and the Holy Spirit. But it never wore off. No, and it never will.

I often think of Campbell. He vanished from his old haunts, and I have not seen him since that night at Angelus Temple. As far as I know, he is still living in that awful hell of addiction.

With all my heart, I would like to make a personal appeal to Campbell—wherever you are:

> Campbell, there is hope for you. I don't know where you are or what you are doing, but I love you. And God loves you. I know He does because He showed His love for me. And if He can love and save me, then I know He wants to do the same thing for you. Campbell, I cannot express the joy, satisfaction, peace, and abundance of life that is mine in Christ. Dope—it is nothing compared to

the power and adventure of the Holy Spirit. God loves you, Campbell, and He wants you to turn your life over to Jesus Christ and be born again. You don't need to attend a Kathryn Kuhlman meeting. You don't need to have her lay hands on you. All you need is Jesus—and He is right beside you right now. Wherever you are, Campbell, if you will just reach up and receive Him, He will come into your heart and change you. Oh, Campbell, come to Him...now.

17

Medically Incurable
by Walter Bennett

*Walter and Naurine Bennett live on the Palos
Verdes Peninsula, southwest of Los Angeles. Both
hold Master's Degrees from the University of South-
ern California. Mr. Bennett is a real estate broker with
offices on Wilshire Boulevard in Beverly Hills. Mrs.
Bennett is Assistant Principal at Leuzinger High
School in Centinela Valley and Dean of the Fine Arts
Department. In 1966, she won the Woman of the Year
award from the Fine Arts Association of Centinela
Valley for furthering art and culture.*

Naurine and I were what you might call typical Baptists. Back in my home town of Paducah, Kentucky, if
you were not a Baptist, you just did not count. So when
I married Naurine, who was a United Brethren from
Sumner, Illinois (a small town in Lawrence County), I
told her she had to become a Baptist, too. "After all," I
kidded her, "you want to get to heaven, don't you?"

We moved to California in 1947 and later we both
enrolled at USC to obtain our Master's Degrees. I taught

in the public school for twelve years before going into the real estate business in Los Angeles. Naurine went into public school administration and has been at the same school for nineteen years. Since we were always active church members, we joined a local Baptist church. However, since Naurine's healing...but I am getting ahead of myself. Let's go back to two days after Thanksgiving in 1954.

I had gotten up early and was in the bathroom shaving when I heard Naurine cry out. I thought she was kidding and sauntered back into the bedroom and jokingly said something about the holidays and old age. Then I saw she was not kidding. Her face was blanched white and her mouth drawn in intense pain. "It's my hip," she gasped, "Something is wrong...."

I tried to get her on her feet, but she cried out in pain and fell back on the bed, unable to stand. I straightened her out on the bed and picked up the phone and called our family physician. "Bring her to my office," he said.

Thirty minutes later, I helped Naurine from the car into the doctor's office. She was unable to stand on her left leg and spoke of excruciating pain in her hip. The doctor examined her and shook his head. "I do not think it is organic," he said. "We need to get her to a specialist."

I agreed, and the doctor called an orthopedic surgeon. We were instructed to meet him at Centinela Hospital in Inglewood immediately.

X-rays showed the hip joint was full of fluid, which had forced the hip out of its socket. The orthopedist took Naurine into surgery, where he inserted a long needle into the back of the joint in an effort to withdraw the fluid. This was unsuccessful, so he tried again from the front. Again, he was unable to withdraw any fluid. The next procedure followed was to put her left leg in heavy traction—and wait.

She remained in traction for three weeks. Every time the weights were removed, the intense pain returned. By that time, the pain was no longer localized in the hip but had spread throughout her body. Besides that, the doctors discovered a large distension in the lower abdominal area as it seemingly filled up with fluid. Her whole system was rapidly becoming affected.

The orthopedist called our own doctor back on the case and indicated he had no success with his treatment. Perhaps, he suggested, the disease was organic after all. Various drugs and medicines were applied, but there was no progress. As a matter of fact, she kept regressing steadily.

A few days before Christmas, I asked the doctors if I could bring her home for the holidays. They agreed and I took her home. She remained unable to get out of bed and the day after New Year's, I came home from school and found her doubled over in pain.

"I have a terrific pulling sensation," she cried as she twisted on the bed, holding her sides. I phoned the doctor and he said I should get her back in the hospital as soon as possible.

This time, she was running a high fever, her blood pressure had dropped to a dangerous level, and the pain had spread throughout her entire body. A team of doctors helped with the examination and tests which indicated there was a general hardening of all the outer tissue on all the internal organs of the body. The same condition was detected in the epidermis of her body, also.

After ten days in the old Methodist Hospital in Los Angeles, our family physician called me into his office. "Walter, there is every evidence that Naurine has a rare disease known as lupus." He paused while I tried to comprehend what he had said. "I do not quite know how to say this," he said, dropping his head, "but I know you are both Christians and have a different outlook on life than some of the others I treat. Still...." His voice trailed off and I felt my heart leap into my throat. "There is just no easy way to say this, Walter," he continued. "The disease is incurable and if we are right in our diagnosis, she will probably never leave the hospital alive."

He had said it. Yet I could not believe my ears. "Incurable...never leave the hospital...."

"No!" I choked out, trying to pull myself to my feet, yet feeling my legs collapse under me. "You have to be wrong."

The doctor came around the desk, where I sat shaking with fear. He put his hand on my shoulder and spoke softly, "Walter, there is a slight chance we are wrong. And we have more tests to run. Maybe they will turn up something different. But your wife is a mighty sick girl and if it is what we think it is, there is just nothing much medical science can do about it."

They did do more tests. They did a biopsy on her thigh, taking a sample of bone, tendon, and several layers of skin and muscle tissue. These were tested by the pathologist who sent his report back to our doctor. The first week in February, the doctor called me back into his office. "Walter, I told you we might be wrong on that first diagnosis. Now it seems that we were. We have positively identified Naurine's condition as scleroderma."

I had the definite feeling that he was trying to let me down easily, give me hope when he knew there was no hope. "What is scleroderma?" I asked.

"It affects the vital organs of the body," he said. "The skin tissues of these organs begin to harden."

"You said the vital organs?" I said, my mouth dry. "Do you mean her heart as well?"

"Yes, her heart, kidneys, liver, and lungs. The coverings on all these organs will get progressively harder and less pliable. This will mean intense pain in every area of the body, but we can give her some comfort...." He paused as if unwilling to continue.

"What is the prognosis?" I whispered, deathly afraid of his answer. "You said lupus was fatal. What about scleroderma?"

The doctor got up from his chair and walked to the window, his back toward me. "Scleroderma is medically incurable, also. It might take a little longer to run its course, but if the medication does its job, she ought to live at least three years." Again he paused and then added, as if talking to himself, "If she can stand the pain that long."

"Three years? My God, I cannot stand this." My thoughts were frantically screaming why, why, why? We had been good people. We belonged to a church. We tithed our income. We were active in the Lord's work. We did not smoke or drink. We prayed and read our Bible. Why would God let this happen to Naurine?

The doctor continued looking out the window. I sensed his deep feeling of inadequacy, not only in the face of this medically incurable disease, but in the face of my intense silence. He did not have any answer. Nor did anyone else seem to have the answer.

The next day, the internist and our doctor came by Naurine's room while I was sitting with her. "Mr. Bennett, there is a research program under way in New York that has shown some results in drug use to retard this disease. It is not a cure and is still in the experimental stage. As a matter of fact, we will have to have your permission to use the drug. However, as it stands now, we have no place else to turn, and I strongly advise you to give us permission to start this treatment at once."

I glanced at Naurine. Her face was twitching in pain and her body trembled. "Yes," I said, "do whatever you can and do it fast. I do not think she can stand much more of this."

The doctor called New York that morning and the new medication was put on a plane for Los Angeles. Treatment began at midnight. The new drug was mixed with glucose to be given intravenously, and drop by drop, it was assimilated by her diseased system.

From the very outset, there was marked improvement in Naurine's condition. At the end of the twenty-seven day period, the intravenous dosage was complete and a comparable medication was administered by mouth. By the middle of April, she had improved enough that the doctor said I could take her home.

The first hospitalization of almost four months was to be, however, only the first of many over the ensuing years. Naurine's improved condition did not last. Every new medication that came our way was tried, but none appeared to help. She was regressing to her original condition and pain.

In desperation, I wrote Mayo Clinic. The physician who replied stated that as there was no definite cure for scleroderma, the only suggestion he could offer was to follow the direction of my own physician. In other words, Mayo said it was hopeless, also.

Naurine had been unable to work for fifteen months. However, the doctor said that inactivity would shorten her life quicker than anything else. She had to keep moving. She had to keep exercising. If not, her muscles would become rigid and she would become bedridden. Therefore, the doctor suggested that she go back to work for two hours a day. A daily injection became necessary.

As the months passed, she began to take the shots at home along with a total of fifty-three pills a day. We knew her heart was being affected—shooting pains flashed down her arms much like those in a heart attack. Kidneys, lungs, eyes, and the skin of her body were becoming more and more affected.

Naurine tried working on a two-hour-a-day basis and increased to a four-hour day after a few months. By September, 1956, almost two years after her first symptoms, she was able to force herself to work a full eight-hour schedule, even though the pain was almost unbearable.

"Keep pushing yourself," the doctor said. "Do not give up, for if you give up, your condition will worsen. You have to keep going."

I realized this and made her get up each morning to get to work. It was a horrible ordeal, for after a night's sleep, the pain in her stiffened muscles was excruciating. The tension mounted. I knew I had to force her, yet I felt like a heel doing it. "I just cannot go on," she would say. But I loved her enough to force her to keep pushing.

The pain grew worse, just as the doctors had said it would. They changed her medicine and put her on three different cortisone derivatives, as well as other prescribed medications as research on the disease released new medication. The daily shots continued, or if she missed one, a double dose the following day.

She had outlived her three years and for that, we were thankful. She had been hospitalized at least twice a year, but she was still going. But it was becoming tougher and tougher each week. At times her muscles would go into spasms and her toes would draw back under her feet and sometimes lock in that position, requiring much massaging to get them to return to normal position. Any exposure to sunlight or heat caused intense pain and accumulation of fluid. Cold baths were all she could stand and as the months staggered past, I had to pack her legs in ice so she could get relief enough to sleep at night.

Conservatively speaking, we had spent close to thirty thousand dollars for medical treatment. Our check stubs showed we had spent more than nineteen thousand dollars for drugs alone over the eleven-year period.

She was determined, by this time, to push on. The one thing she was not going to become was an invalid. "I may die on my feet, but I will not be confined to bed," she said stubbornly. God knows how much I admired her spunk and fighting spirit, for there were times when I saw her climbing steps that caused such pain in her muscles that the tears splashed on her clothes. But she kept going. Always before her was the specter of a bedridden life due to rigidity of muscles and organs, so she gritted her teeth and struggled on. Even when sitting, she was moving her arms and legs, neck and head, even fingers and toes—always moving.

In November, 1965, eleven years after the first attack, Naurine was hospitalized for the last time. Large, liver-colored spots had begun to appear on her legs and hips, two to three inches in diameter. The doctors did a series of tests and said the disease had reached its final stage of progression. There was nothing medically they could do any more except wait for the end.

But the end was much different than the doctors predicted.

On December 15, a Lutheran friend called to tell Naurine about a new book she had just discovered: *I Believe in Miracles*. She was going to bring it by the house for us to read.

We read it together. Spiritual healing had just never been my cup of tea. As a matter of fact, we had never been to a miracle service in our entire lives. Surely, as a Bible-believing Baptist, I believed that God could heal sick bodies. The difference was that I had never believed that God actually did it today. Healing today is done by the doctors and hospitals, I had thought. We had not been taught about the healing ministry of the Holy Spirit. But now I was suddenly confronted with the possibility that God still worked miracles—bypassing regular means, at times, to perform healing himself.

"Could it actually be true?" we wondered out loud. We were soon to find out.

After Christmas, which we both thought would be Naurine's last, her Lutheran friend called again. Miss Kuhlman would be speaking at the Shrine Auditorium on January 23. She asked Naurine to go with her.

I had been in bed with a bad case of flu, but decided that we should both go. So we skipped church and drove across town to attend the miracle service, taking our Lutheran friend and two other ladies with us.

We had been warned to arrive early and were glad we did. The doors did not open that Sunday until 1 P.M., but when we arrived at 10:30 A.M., there were at least a thousand people already crowded around the huge portico outside the auditorium.

We wedged ourselves as close to the door as possible. Our Lutheran friend, knowing the situation, had advised us to take a camp stool for Naurine. After she sat down, the four of us formed a little circle around her, holding hands, to keep the crowd from pressing against her pain-wracked body.

At one o'clock, the doors opened and we were swept into the building ahead of the almost stampeding mass of humanity. We finally found seats on the main floor about halfway down in the center of the auditorium. I glanced at Naurine. Her face was pale from pain. Her body was quivering with the characteristic mannerisms she had developed to keep all the muscles moving. She constantly crossed and recrossed her legs, moved her arms, and wiggled her fingers.

"Are you all right?" I whispered. She gave me a smile and nodded her head.

We were skeptical, to say the least. As the meeting got underway and I saw people coming to the platform claiming they had been healed of various maladies, my skepticism grew worse, until a strange thing happened which I could not doubt.

Sitting next to me was a woman who had been wheezing badly from asthma. Earlier, she had asked me to help her out if her wheezing got too bad. About halfway through the service, the woman suddenly began to tremble and stood to her feet, clutching her throat. I thought she was having an attack and started to stand to help her when I realized she was crying. "I have been healed," she said, looking at me. "I can breathe. I am not wheezing anymore. Something has happened in my chest." Her voice rose in excitement as she repeatedly said, "I am healed. I am healed."

One of the workers hurried down the side and took the woman to the platform to share her testimony. I could hardly believe it and knew that my eyes were as round as saucers. I slumped back down in my seat in stunned silence. "What is going on here?" I asked Naurine. "Did you see that?"

I began to pray, "Dear God, if You really do heal people today, please heal Naurine. Touch her body and heal her." It was a pretty weak prayer, but it was all I could choke out. Still, nothing happened. I glanced at my watch and saw that it was almost 5 P.M. We had been there six and a half hours. I knew the service was drawing to a close. "I guess nothing is going to happen after all," I murmured to myself.

Just then, Miss Kuhlman left the line of those who had come forward to testify of their healings and walked back to the center microphone. She said, "The presence of the Holy Spirit is so great in this auditorium at this moment that anyone can receive anything he desires from the Lord by just reaching up and receiving it from Him. Sing with me." And the choir and congregation burst into song with the words and music of *He Touched Me*.

I turned and looked at Naurine. Her face was uplifted toward heaven and she had both hands extended above her head, palms up, as if she were waiting to receive something from God himself.

And then she did. The countenance on her face changed as if there were a heavenly light glowing around her head and shoulders. Her eyes filled with tears and an almost angelic smile came to her lips. Her body began to tremble. It started with the top of her head in what she later described as a tremendous, but painless, jolt of electricity. Her whole body was quivering and suddenly her head was thrown forward to her knees in what I thought was a giant spasm.

I could hear Miss Kuhlman's voice above the singing, "Someone in this center section, right down here, has just been healed of a rare skin disease. Where is that person?"

I sensed that Naurine was trying to stand, but she was still shaking violently. Her whole muscular and nervous system seemed to be taking its commands from some other circuit than her brain waves. She kept trying to stand but could not. Four times Miss Kuhlman called out for the person to stand before Naurine finally straightened to her feet. She was the one. She had been healed.

"Honey, did you faint?" I asked her.

She looked at me with wide eyes as she held onto the back of the seat in front of her. She was swaying and I was afraid she would fall. "I don't know what has happened to me, but the pain...the pain is gone. Walter! The pain is gone," she said with joy and unbelief. "I don't hurt anymore."

She fell back into her seat under what I now know was the power of God. An usher who had been attending our section, a man whom we later discovered was a Presbyterian elder, approached us and asked us to step out into the aisle. Between the two of us, we helped Naurine to her feet and to the stage. She was coherent but reeling and staggering like a drunken person. She had been healed, totally and completely!

Immediately, things began to happen. Naurine stopped taking her medicine. All fifty-three pills and the daily shot were left behind. I knew from my limited medical background that if the cortisone drugs were withdrawn without tapering off that the patient would usually go into a coma. However, Naurine was insistent that God had purged her body of all traces of the disease and drugs and refused to take a single pill. She has never taken a pill since that day.

Neither of us slept during the next three days. It was as if we were living in a dream world. We were both so excited over what had taken place that when night came we turned on all the lights and stayed up, talking and listening to the stereo and praising God.

A very odd thing was taking place, too. During this three day period of time, Naurine's body was extremely warm, almost hot. She had no apparent fever, but the skin over her entire body felt like a warm light bulb, almost too hot to touch. At the end of the third day, it went away and she felt her body returning to its normal temperature. That night, we both fell into bed exhausted and slept around the clock.

Within a week, she called her doctor for an appointment. He asked her to go to the clinic for laboratory tests. He would have his nurse set up an appointment for her examination when he received the results of her tests. She had not even so much as hinted that she had been healed. She wanted to surprise him.

She did. On February 22, the doctor called and asked us both to come to his office. His nurse asked me to wait in his waiting room while he examined Naurine. After the examination, he sat back on his stool near the examining table and said, "All right, Mrs. Bennett, tell me what happened."

"What do you mean?" she asked, trying to hold back her smiles.

"You know what I mean. Something has happened. When I examined you just now, I found no symptoms of scleroderma in your body. And besides," he said, opening her huge medical folder, "these last tests from the lab are all negative. Now tell me what happened."

Naurine asked, "Do you believe in miracles?"

"Yes, I do," he said. "I have seen too much happen that cannot be explained scientifically to discredit the power of God." She then related what had taken place. He just sat there and listened. When she had finished, he said, "What about your medicine?"

"I've stopped it," she said.

"Even the cortisone?"

"Four weeks ago—on the day of my healing," she said, with a firm smile on her face.

"I see," he mused. "When you finish dressing, you may wait in the outer room. I will be out shortly."

He left the examination room and came directly to his waiting room where I was sitting and invited me into his office. "I have just finished examining your wife, Walter. Maybe you can tell me what has happened to her," he said casually.

Not knowing that Naurine had just told him the complete story, I started at the beginning and gave him the full account of the miracle service. When I finished he sat silently behind his desk for a brief moment. "What about the drugs?" he said. "She is still taking her cortisone, isn't she?"

"Oh, no," I answered, "she stopped that along with all the other drugs four weeks ago—the day of her healing."

He declared that Naurine's healing could be classified under one category only: miracle. He added, "Do not try to explain it—just accept it and live a normal life."

We have not missed a Kathryn Kuhlman service at the Shrine since that time. We still are and probably always will be Baptists. But I do not think that anyone will ever again tag us as "typical."

18

"Comrade" with Christ

by E.A. Pereszlenyi, M.D.

*His eyes were piercing, but a more kindly face I
perhaps shall never see. The first time I met him was
in the sanctuary of the First Presbyterian Church in
Pittsburgh, Pennsylvania. Dr. Pereszlenyi did not
know until sometime later that it was the same church
which Dr. Clarence McCartney had pastored for twen-
ty-six years. One of the latter's best sermons had been
translated from English into Hungarian by Dr. Pereszlenyi while he was still living in Hungary.*

*Dr. Pereszlenyi is in General Practice in Toron-
to, Ontario, Canada. He was born in Mochacs, Hungary, in 1919, and holds a medical degree from the
University of Pecs. During World War II, he was a
medic and after the communist takeover, he served in
the Hungarian army as a medical officer. In September, 1958, he defected to the free world. Later he was
admitted to Canada where he took additional training
at Hamilton General Hospital and then was granted
a Fellowship in Cardiology at the Hospital for Sick*

Children in Toronto. Five years after the doctor left communist Hungary, his fiancee, Julia, was allowed to join him and they were married in Hamilton.

There is no room for God in the communist society. Communism, it is claimed, feeds, clothes, and provides for the people, and in a sense it provides the equivalent of what Christians know as "the way, the truth, and the life." God, therefore, is irrelevant.

I was fortunate enough to escape such a society, and I shall share with you some of my experiences as a Christian doctor behind the iron curtain. I shall also tell of my search in the institutional churches of the free world for a recognition of the real God.

I hope, as you share my background, you will better understand my enthusiasm on discovering the Kathryn Kuhlman ministry where God is recognized and worshiped as the God of miracles—where He and He alone is given the glory as the Great Provider, the Great Saviour, and the Great Physician.

The communist regime has established the most elaborate system of surveillance the world has ever seen. Someone is always watching. In every apartment house, there is a Committee of Tenantry which is supervised by the block warden. In every office, store, and factory, there is a Works Committee, which (though an organ of the Trade Union) is in fact the simple tool of the Communist Party. Everywhere there is the Basic Party Organization whose secretary is lord over the living. Nothing of any consequence may happen without his consent. Finally, there is the Political Police who hold the authority to arrest anyone, even a minister of the government.

At the root of this entire system of oppression are the informers, without whom the system could not function. Every man, woman, boy, and girl under the communist regime is expected to be an informer and, as we have seen, organized groups of informers are strategically placed in every apartment house, factory, office, and business.

The "Party" is constantly offering favors and rewards to those who will inform on their neighbors or even their own families. Everyone is expendable. If a man is accused of being a reactionary, he is relegated to the most insignificant type of job. Large numbers of prisoners were sent to work camps in Siberia or even to Red China to spend their remaining years in miserable surroundings. Human life is useful only as it works for the Party.

Thus, you see, in such a society where God is ignored, where the printing and even the reading of the Bible is hindered in every possible way, where man is expected to inform on his own father or mother to receive a favor from the almighty Party—life for the Christian can be quite perilous.

Hungary has not always been a communist nation. In a series of tragic diplomatic blunders, she became the pawn of the victors following the two great wars. A helpless maiden, she was thrust into the cell of political rapists. I was an escapee from the old army because I did not want to retreat to Germany at the time my country was handed over to the communists after World War II. Although we cringed in fear at the prospect of becoming Russia's slaves, such are the fortunes of war. Our people had been bartered into hell by the infamous stroke of a pen on the Yalta Treaty.

I was converted to Christ sometime between six and seven o'clock in the morning on the third of July, 1940.

I was a medical school student at the University of Pecs. For three years I had been diligently reading my Bible, but I had never fully accepted Jesus. The night of my conversion, I could not sleep and before dawn I got up and walked in the park, praying and praying for God to reveal himself to me. Just before the sun came up, the Person of Jesus became very real to me—and I knew—I knew that He died for my sin. I accepted Him that morning as my Lord and Saviour.

In 1945, following the war, I returned to Pecs. There, as a young intern, I was exposed to extreme pressure (as were all students, interns, and doctors) to join the Communist Party. Lenin had written in one of his books that doctors should be "evangelists" for the cause of communism, and at least ninety percent of the Hungarian doctors at Pecs had already joined the party. I was offered rewards and a lucrative position if I, too, would join.

I realized, however, that communism was not the remedy for society's ills anymore than cholera can be cured by the plague. I knew that Jesus Christ alone was the answer for the world's ills, and I intended to be a "comrade" with Him alone.

Dr. Istvan Kenesse, a prominent member of the Communist Party Organization of Doctors, warned that my "hesitation" to join the Party would be overlooked no longer. Within three months, I was compelled to leave my position as an intern at the University Hospital in Pecs. Dr. Lajos Rostas, my chief and a trustee of the Communist Party, had written a three-page letter accusing me of being a reactionary on the basis that I read my Bible every day, a brand which I was powerless to remove. As is often the case in communism, a short time later Dr. Rostas was expelled from the party and lost his job at the University.

236

Fortunately for me, the Secretary of the Alliance of the Communist Trade Unions in Pecs became sincerely concerned about my future. The previous year, I had dissuaded his wife from committing suicide and when he heard of my situation, he helped me obtain a residency in the Bajcsy-Zsilinszky Hospital in Budapest. God's promise to me was fulfilled: "The rod of the wicked shall not rest upon the lot of the righteous..." (Psalm 125:3).

One evening, one of my old patients, a Roman Catholic, was dying and she wished to see a priest. In order to allow a priest to enter the hospital, the dying patient had to apply for an approval and the resident on call had to sign it. The priest came and I whispered to one of the nurses, "There is another dying patient in the ward. Let the priest hear her confession also."

Early the next morning I was called to the office of the Secretary of the Party Organization in the hospital. The entire Executive Committee was present, along with a typist to take down my statement. "What happened last night?" the secretary asked.

"What do you mean?"

"About the priest," he replied.

I knew I was in big trouble, but the Lord took over and guided my tongue as I answered. "There was an old woman dying. If I refused to let the priest come, the rest of the people in the ward (and there were about twenty people in that ward) would have said there was no freedom of religion in Hungary. I was working in the interest of the People's Democracy by letting him come to prove we honor everyone's constitutional rights."

The men all turned and looked at one another and nodded. I was allowed to return to my job on the floor.

Dr. Galocsi, a leading communist and my chief in the Bajcsy-Zsilinszky Hospital realized I was a trustworthy and hard-working man. In spite of the fact that I was a Christian, he made an effort to change my political standing. In the fall of 1950, I was drafted into the medical center of the Air Force doing specialist work. However, when the political department of the Air Force learned I was a Christian, they decided to transfer me to the army because they considered me "not reliable." After a series of transfers from one military post to another, I was finally assigned to a military engineering camp at Midszent on the Yugoslavian frontier in the capacity of medical officer.

One morning, one of the soldiers appeared at the office with dysentery. I was panic-stricken. Only a few months before, Major Dr. Szanto had been hanged in Tata because the soldiers under his care had contracted diarrhea. Apparently the communists believed that through fear they could force doctors to do their best. In fact, the fear pervaded all the professions. If a building collapsed or settled on its foundations, they would hang the architect or engineer—a threat to all others that they had better not make the same mistake.

Over the following days, several more soldiers reported to my tent with dysentery. An epidemic was breaking out. In despair I began to pray and called on some Christian friends to pray for me. The epidemic grew worse and the surgeon of the Army Corps came to inspect the camp. I told him the problems resulted from poor sanitation. He looked at me for a long time. "All right, Comrade lieutenant, I make you a dictator. Anything you say about health is law. Even the commanding officer must obey you."

God blessed our efforts, and our sanitary conditions improved so marvelously that I received a citation from the surgeon general for stopping the epidemic among the soldiers at Mindszent. (However, the citation never reached me since it was intercepted by the Political Department of the Ministry of Defense who thought this too great an honor for a "clerical," the repugnant stigma borne by those who attend church in Hungary.) As a result of this good work, though, I was transferred to the Crack Division (the best in the country) in Kalocsa. There I was to be the commanding officer of the hospital of the division.

Every commanding officer had a counterpart, a political officer. I knew such a man would be arriving as my constant companion—to live in my tent with me and spy on me. My political "comrade" was young and ambitious and I had no doubt that he hoped to prove his alertness and be promoted if he could find cause for my imprisonment. However, I determined I would not back down from my convictions. On the night of his arrival, I said, "Since my nineteenth year, I have been reading my Bible. I hope you will not mind if I continue this practice. After all, this is my personal tent."

A faint smile spread over his face. "That's fine, Comrade, go right ahead." I sensed then that my days were numbered.

My political companion's zeal knew no bounds. He was determined to prove I was an agent of the "American Imperialists." My suitcase was often searched in my absence and all my conversations carefully weighed. Every shred of evidence that could be used against me was put into a file. Though such oppression was constant, I gained strength from my daily Bible readings from the little Moravian Bible Guide that I used then and still do.

239

One verse in particular comforted me during those times. "And they shall fight against thee; but they shall not prevail..." (Jeremiah 1:19). And they did not.

It was about this time that another influence entered my life—Julia. I met her in Budapest when I was taking a course for senior administrative medical officers. Though despised as a "clerical," my work was so much appreciated and I was so valued as a medical officer that I was among the first sixteen who were chosen for this course. I was the only non-member of the Communist Party.

Julia and I saw a good bit of each other and I found out she was a believer in spiritual healing. I, too, knew from the Bible that spiritual healing was possible, but felt that much of the church could no longer claim this gift due to its lost estate and frailty. Suffering, I had been told, is a part of life and something to be endured. It should not be prayed away. This, my friends tried to make me believe, also applied to my own oppression as a Christian in the communist army. When you are oppressed there is nothing you do about it but bear it, I was repeatedly told.

I was told this by all of my friends except Julia. "No," she said, "God does not want you to suffer. He wants to lift your burden."

"I have always been told that it makes a man strong to suffer," I replied. But Julia's logic made sense, I had to admit. It was what the Bible taught and I believed the Bible. I began to think she was right. I could actually pray for release from the military service so I could practice medicine without restriction. I was encouraged and my hope began to take roots and grow.

Life in the communist army remained unbearable. Unwilling to have me exterminated merely on the grounds that I was a Christian, they tried to find some fault with my medical work. Everything I did was under close scrutiny. However, through God's grace, the hospital was judged most highly in the military service. This time the citation was given to my counterpart—the political officer.

Because of my religious beliefs, eventually I was sent to Budapest on "compulsory vacation," which amounted to open arrest. My pay was withheld and I was forbidden to practice medicine because I was still a part of the army. I was followed constantly. When I walked down the street, I was always aware that someone was following me. When I stopped, he stopped. When I turned, he turned. At night I could peek out my apartment window and see him on the sidewalk below. I had one satisfaction, however—attending a preaching mission at a famous Lutheran church. This meant the spy had to attend, too. What a sense of humor God must have, I thought, as I glanced across the church and saw that poor fellow sitting there and listening to the Gospel because of his assignment—me!

My "compulsory vacation" lasted two months. I had received no pay in that time and I had gradually used up all my savings and realized that I soon would face starvation. One night I boarded a local bus, paying the fare with my last few cents, and encountered the army corps surgeon. He shook his head when he saw me.

"What did you do, Comrade lieutenant? Why did you do it?" he asked.

"All I have done is my job," I said.

"Oh, no, there are eight testimonies against you. They say you spoke about religion."

"But I never started any conversation on religious matters," I said. "I only answered questions that were asked of me. I never went to church in my uniform. I cannot see what bad things I have done to deserve this."

"Nonetheless, things look very dark for you, Comrade," he said. "Very dark."

Frightened, I returned to my apartment. My Bible reading for the day was still open before me. "So Daniel was taken up out of the den, and no manner of hurt was found upon him, because he believed in God." If God could shut the mouths of lions, He could also handle the communist bear, I thought. I took fresh courage from the Word.

In June, 1953, there was a big change in the communist policy. Stalin had been dead three months and the "melting" reached into Hungary, and for one single week, Hungary seemed to be free under a new prime minister. I was ordered to the Ministry of Defense where they almost apologized for my treatment and I received all my back pay. During this week, the decision was made for my release from the army. My record was clean and I was dismissed and classified as "professionally and politically blameless." I was free!

At least I thought I was free until I returned to Budapest and found that no doctor discharged from the army could practice medicine in the capitol. He was considered a poor political risk. I had been set free from one chain and bound with another. I made up my mind to escape from the country as soon as I could.

Julia and I continued seeing each other, and I spent much time studying English. In spite of the fact that I was considered a poor political risk, God intervened once again and I received a very fine appointment to take further training in internal medicine and later in cardiology in one of the best hospitals in the city.

My evenings were spent doing translations from English into Hungarian, translating not only Dr. Clarence McCartney's sermon, "Come Before Winter," but the entire manuscript of Billy Graham's *Peace With God* and Torrey's *How To Pray*. The translations had to be handwritten, but then later were typed and passed around secretly among the Christians.

Then came October 23, 1956....

The chairwoman came running into my office and screamed that I should go to the window. Below were thousands of Hungarian men and youth, marching down the street, waving banners and shouting "Russians go home!" It was the revolution.

We were all taken by surprise. There had been great unrest among the Hungarian people, but we had no idea that so many thousands and thousands of young people were willing to pay with their lives for the cause of freedom. One of my friends with political connections confided to me that the entire revolution had been instigated by the Russians, to make the Hungarians force their hand so that all rebels could be liquidated—and that was exactly what happened.

The fighting lasted three days and then the Russians withdrew to the perimeter of the city. As a former military officer, I knew what was coming. I knew they were bringing up the tanks. Inside Budapest freedom reigned, but it was like the eye of a hurricane. On the morning of November 4, the rumble of tanks was heard in the streets. The Hungarian Army and the Freedom Fighters attempted the impossible: fighting the tanks with guns and grenades. But it was hopeless.

The tanks slaughtered the men by the thousands and the streets were strewn with the dead and dying. The tanks mercilessly punished the slightest resistance, destroying whole apartment buildings for one single gun shot. The slaughter by the Nazis was almost humane compared to the treatment by the Russians. We kept waiting for help to come from the free nations—but none came. Tens of thousands were slaughtered and the streets turned red with blood. At night the trucks would patrol the streets, picking up the corpses and taking them to mass graves in the cemeteries.

The hospital staff worked night and day trying to save thousands who had been dragged in, wounded and maimed. Any reservations I had about defecting to the free world were all wiped away during those days of hell. Even Julia, who had been opposed to leaving Hungary, was now encouraging me. She promised to follow as soon as she could.

My problem was how to get out. The border to the west was heavily guarded. About one hundred kilometers from the border, all papers were checked and none but residents of the area were even permitted to enter the frontier zone. Extending from the Austrian border were kilometer after kilometer of guard towers, all equipped with bright searchlights, telephone connections, and machine guns. All the guards carried submachine guns and patrolled the areas between the towers with bloodhounds specially trained to capture anyone who might venture into the area. Signal wires, camouflaged to look like plant runners, would set off alarm bells in the towers when touched, and rows of land mines were buried in the earth along the border. All this was enclosed by three rows of barbed-wire entanglements. These barriers, of course, did much to dissuade me from trying to defect across the border.

Then, early in 1958, I applied for permission to participate in the Third World Congress of Cardiology to be held in Brussels. I was afraid that because of my past record I would be turned down, yet God was working. The door opened and I received my passport to attend. The time had come to leave the land of my birth forever.

Even though we could not announce it publicly, Julia and I pledged our love to each other. One week later, September 12, 1958, I left Hungary and when I arrived in Brussels, I stepped into the police station and asked for political asylum. It would be five years before I would see Julia again. In Brussels, days turned to months, but eventually I was granted immigration to Canada. I took resident work at Hamilton General Hospital in cardiology at the Hospital for Sick Children in Toronto.

The political police in Hungary repeatedly rejected Julia's application for an exit permit until she began to pray together with her friends. A miraculous chain of events were set in motion, for suddenly a prominent politician obtained the document that allowed her to emigrate to Belgium. The Belgians, however, refused to grant her an immigrant visa because I could not provide any guarantee that she would be subsequently admitted to Canada. The adamant position of the Belgian Ministry of Justice changed, however, when a personal friend of the attaché requested the visa. As I worked in Canada to bring Julia to Toronto, a new Minister of Immigration and an impending general election finally removed the Canadian objections. I met Julia at the ship in Montreal on July 12, 1963, and we were married.

Julia and I were completely happy to be together again. We had found the long-awaited freedom our hearts yearned for under Communist rule, but Julia's health was not good. I became increasingly alarmed about her. She had a bad inflammation of the gall bladder and possible stones. She had a recurring infection of the kidneys and I knew her appendix was in bad shape—very elongated and surrounded with serious adhesions. She had an ulcerated colon accompanied by extensive bleeding. I was concerned because she would not take medicine. She reacted violently even to children's doses. It seemed I could treat everyone but my own wife.

Our frustrations deepened as we sought for a church in which to worship and serve. While in Hamilton, a dear pastor had helped prepare me to find my way in the jungle of liberal and confused theology that prevails in much of the free world. In Hungary, we had always been able to find Christian friends who believed and with whom we could find fellowship in prayer. But here...?

The longing for Christian fellowship and love became a terrific burden upon our hearts. We felt even more lonely in the free world than we had under communist oppression. There the people knew what it cost to be a Christian. We knew that any moment the political police could knock at the door and take us all to jail; it was a matter of life and death. Here, however, living was so easy, so free of restraint on beliefs, that religious worship seemed abstract, lacking reality and personal meaningfulness.

No one really seemed to understand our loneliness, our longing for Christian fellowship without the trappings of a complex organization. "Back in Hungary, prayer meetings were necessary," we were told, "because you were under oppression. But here you are free. You don't need to gather for prayer and Bible study in your home. Here you can go to church on Sunday and attend the scheduled services and that is enough. There is no need for more."

As our confusion grew, Julia's health problem became more acute. Though the pain would not keep her in bed, she was constantly beset by suffering. I treated her the best I could, but no medical help seemed to make any difference.

Then some Hungarian friends gave Julia a newspaper clipping from the Toronto Daily Star that told something of the Pittsburgh ministry of Kathryn Kuhlman. The article gave a brief description of the miracle services that were being conducted at the First Presbyterian Church in downtown Pittsburgh. Our friends were planning to attend; Julia went with them. This was our introduction to a ministry that has changed our entire outlook on life and brought not only hope for the future but health for the body.

Because of my medical practice I could not attend that October 18 meeting. Julia, however, returned and recounted in great detail the marvelous miracles she had seen. "I have read books," she said, "about the great German healers of the last century; but in Pittsburgh, I saw miracles happening before my very eyes."

Never had I seen Julia more vibrant and enthusiastic. "My greatest impression was the love. The healings were marvelous, but it was the love and acceptance that I felt that made me know this was the answer to our search."

My excitement beginning to match hers and I asked Julia countless questions. "Miss Kuhlman gives all the glory to God. She is not like others who try to claim some of the glory. She gives it all to God," Julia said. "And such tenderness. It makes no difference what your race, she loves all people. If she loves all races, then surely she loves Hungarians also."

I nodded my head. "Yes, this must be the place for us." By now I, too, believed this was God's work and I promised Julia I would take her to Pittsburgh to attend another miracle service. I invited George, a young patient of mine, to go with us—he had been stricken by a rare case of cerebral multiple sclerosis (MS of the brain). Thursday, December 5, we drove to Pittsburgh to attend the meeting the following day at the Presbyterian Church—Julia, young George, his father, and I.

The youth had to be led into the auditorium and propped up in one of the pews. Julia's pains were severe, but not so bad that she could not walk. The tingle of excitement of preparing to see the power of God in action was almost more than I could stand. Even as I entered that spacious auditorium, I knew I had found the answer to my long search.

The service had barely gotten underway when Miss Kuhlman said, "Somebody is being healed of an intestinal condition." Julia stood to her feet beside me. She was trembling and crying. I stood with her, tears in my eyes. The power of God came down upon her that hour. Miss Kuhlman prayed for Julia and the glory of God rested upon her. Never in all her life had she felt such power, such love, such glory.

Julia reached out and touched the youth's shoulder with her fingertips. The glory was still on her and I could literally see an unbelievable improvement in his body. I knew. I knew that finally I had tapped the source of power of the universe. It was to be found in the Holy Spirit. All those years, I knew He was there. All those years under communist oppression, He had been leading and protecting me. But that morning in Pittsburgh,

I acknowledged Him and became a part of all He wants to do in this world.

Julia's pain has disappeared and her bleeding has stopped completely. My young patient also continues to show evidence of the healing power of God.

Some of my medical colleagues have suggested that if God is the Great Healer, then there is no use for the medical profession anymore. I disagree. I am called of God to practice medicine. I prescribe drugs and refer patients to surgery or specialists when necessary. However, now I also realize that there is a prayer ministry that must go hand in hand with the practice of medicine. Often, from my office, I phone my wife to ask her to pray for a patient whom I cannot help, for now I know that what medicine cannot do, God can do. With Him, nothing is impossible.

Yes, I believe that God gives some persons special gifts to be used in spiritual healing. Just as I refer many of my patients to specialists, I now have no reservation about referring those who cannot be helped by medicine to the greatest Specialist of all—the Great Physician, Jesus Christ.

Look Everyone, I'm Walking

By Mary Pettigrew

With legs to take me where I'd go
With eyes to see the sunset's glow -
With ears to hear what I would know
O God, forgive me when I whine.
I'm blessed indeed. The world is mine!
                                        —Dot Aaron

Clarence and Mary Pettigrew moved back to their
home town of Cobden, Ontario, Canada, in 1954 from
Virginiatown in the northern section of the Province.
They opened a small restaurant and service station on
Highway 17 in the little town of Cobden (population
900) and lived above the business with their three chil-
dren. In 1962 their little world was shaken when
Mary fell victim of a strange malady.

Canada in January is a wonderland of glittering ice
and sparkling snow. Every inch of the brown earth is
covered with a soft blanket of thick whiteness. Fields and

roads, streets and yards, all blend into an endless one-ness beneath the silent quilt of winter.

Muskrat Lake, which stretched the length of the town on the opposite side of the highway to Ottawa, had been frozen over for more than a month. It was spotted with small fishing shacks which had been pulled out on the ice to protect the fishermen from the cold winter air. Cars and skimobiles moved across its frozen surface. It was quite a contrast from the summer months when the green grass sloped gently down to the lapping blue waters and roaring motorboats and spraying water skiers flashed up and down its peaceful surface.

In Cobden, as in most Canadian towns, the principal winter sport is curling. The curling arena becomes the center of community activity as the townspeople gather each evening to participate in the sport. The long lanes, looking much like bowling alleys or inside shuffleboard courts, are covered with a thin coating of ice. Men and women take turns scooting heavy, polished stones toward scoring brackets on the other end of the lanes, much like shuffleboard. Others, on the same team, frantically sweep the ice in front of the gliding rocks with little brooms trying to slow them down or speed them up.

It was at the curling arena when I first noticed something was wrong. I was in my mid-thirties—healthy, vivacious, and full of fun and life. I had always been able to swing the heavy, forty-pound stones into position and scoot them down the lane without difficulty. But that night I was unable to keep my balance and fell several times on the ice.

The next week I was constantly aware of a weakness in my legs. My feet felt as if they were swollen although they looked perfectly normal. I had the sensation at times that they were so big, I could not get them through the doorway. I was waking up in the morning as exhausted as when I went to bed. Clarence insisted that I go to the doctor, but the preliminary examination showed nothing wrong. I was puzzled and confused over the strange and growing symptoms.

We had a fire in the restaurant earlier in the year and were doing much of the remodeling ourselves, but my legs did not allow me to be much help. I was having trouble picking up my feet. Even trying to step over a loose board caused me to trip and go sprawling. I had a lot of falls before I was finally forced to admit that something was wrong.

It happened in July. The Orange Lodges in the area were all getting together for a big parade, or "Orange Walk," on July 12. People from all over the area had arrived for the gala weekend and the little restaurant and service station were doing a booming business.

It was 2:30 A.M. when we finally got out of the restaurant and started up the stairs to our home above the shop. Clarence had just locked the garage and was coming up behind me. "I just don't think I can make it," I gasped about halfway up.

"Come on, dear," he said, giving me a gentle shove from behind. "You are just getting a mite old, that is all."

The next morning I was feeling awful. I was so tired that I could not move out of the bed. Clarence was up dressing to go downstairs and open the station. "Clarence, I am so tired, I can't move."

"Well, why not sleep in for a while," he said.

I knew I would be needed in the restaurant, so I rolled over to drag myself out of bed. But I could not sit up. My left leg would not move. I stared at it, trying mentally to make it move. But it just lay there like a fence post. I started to cry. "Clarence, I've taken a stroke or something. My leg won't move."

"Mary, you must be kidding," he said, but I could sense the anxiety in his voice.

The leg would not move. It was just there. Clarence phoned Dr. Pye and he said to rush me to the hospital in Pembroke. I was there for three weeks, going through one series of tests after another: X-ray, spinal tap, etc. The strange symptoms grew worse. I could stand up, but my left leg simply would not respond. The only way I could walk was by trailing it—taking a step with my right foot and then dragging my left leg behind me.

The doctor finally said, "I am going to let you go home, but I am making immediate plans for you to go to Ottawa to see Dr. Embry, a specialist." We spent that night at home and the next morning Clarence drove me to Ottawa. "A specialist...," I thought to myself as we drove the scenic road from Cobden to Ottawa, "there must be something seriously wrong."

Dr. Embry gave me a thorough examination and then took me back to his office. "Are you alone?" he asked as he sat down behind his desk.

"No, my husband is in the waiting room," I said.

"Better bring him in here," he said, leafing through my file.

I got scared. "What is he going to tell me," I asked myself, quivering with fear. I went to the door and motioned for Clarence. He came in and stood behind my chair. The doctor looked up at me, "Did your doctor not give you any idea about your condition?"

"No," I said, feeling chill bumps run up and down my arms and neck, "he just told me what to do."

He shifted his gaze to Clarence. "Did he not talk to you?"

I looked up at Clarence. He looked at me and then shifted his gaze to the floor. "Yes," he admitted.

"Did he say it was multiple sclerosis?"

There was a long period of silence and then I heard Clarence's weak voice reply, "Yes."

If he had picked up a rock and hit me on the head it would not have hurt so much. I began to cry (which I thought I would never do in front of a doctor), but Dr. Embry just reached in his drawer and handed me a box of tissue. "Go ahead and cry. There would be something wrong with you if you did not."

We sat and talked for a long time afterward. He told me what to expect. The condition would never be any better. It would get progressively worse. So far, they had no cure for it. I could expect to become a cripple. It could be years—or just months.

"I am just laying it on the line, Mrs. Pettigrew," he said. "It is your life that is involved and I would be derelict in my duty if I did not tell you the whole truth. But unless research comes up with a cure, this is the life you will have to adjust yourself to from now on."

I was not very good company on the way home from Ottawa that afternoon. We had three children: Barry was fourteen, Ona was fifteen, and Murray was sixteen. "I do not want to tell the children," I told Clarence.

"You will have to tell them something," he said. "And we cannot lie to them. They are going to find out sooner or later. We might as well tell them the truth."

We did. Their questions were normal teen-age questions. "How long will it be before you are better?"

"I do not know and neither does the doctor," I said. I was grateful they did not seem too disturbed.

I dragged my leg around all summer—up and down the long flight of stairs from our living room to the res-

255

taurant below. By the time the leaves started to change, I was facing the fact I would probably be like this the rest of my life. Autumn had always been my favorite season—the bright sunshine beaming through the nippy air, the hillsides ablaze with reds, golds, greens, and browns. But this fall everything seemed dull—drab. Then I had my second attack.

It happened at the funeral service for my uncle in the little United Church in Forester's Falls. Clarence was a pallbearer and the boys were carrying flowers. Ona and I had taken our seats in the church, but the moment I sat down, I knew something was happening to me. I was losing the power in my whole body. I sensed that my muscles were going completely out of control, although I still had all my mental faculties. It was the oddest feeling, as though I were standing outside myself looking on, powerless to control what my muscles were doing. I began to shake—not just shiver, but shake.

My head was jerking violently back and forth, then sideways. I was afraid my neck would snap. My whole body was bouncing up and down on the pew. Ona was terrified. She had never seen anyone in such shape—nor had I. I kept thinking, what on earth am I going to do? This is like a bad dream.

Then I became aware that Ona was holding onto me—trying to hold me still. But the shaking seemed to get more violent; it seemed that everyone in the church was staring at me, but I was utterly helpless to do anything about it.

Ona was tugging on me, trying to get up so she could get me outside. "I cannot move. I cannot stand up," I said through chattering teeth. She sat back down and put her arms around my body trying to hold me still until the funeral was over.

As the people began to file out, my brother passed by and glanced down where I was sitting. He immediately realized what was happening to me and reached over and pulled me to my feet. Although it was impossible for me to walk, he just put his big arms around my waist and helped me to the door where he simply picked me up in his arms and carried me down the steps.

Clarence was helping the boys with the flowers and looked up at us from the street. He had both arms loaded with flowers and could only give me a helpless, frantic look. The boys, Barry and Murray, were much less inhibited by proper procedure and throwing their flowers on the hoods of several parked cars, they dashed to where I was. They opened the back door of our car and gently placed me on the seat.

"Just leave me alone and go on to the cemetery," I said. But they took me straight on to my aunt's house in Forester's Falls and after the burial Clarence came and took me home. Dr. Pye gave me pills to try to make the shaking subside. The boys sat on my lap to try to hold me down. Nothing worked. That night I could not sleep for shaking. It took two days for it to subside. When it did, I had lost all sensation from my waist down and was unable to stand or walk.

Dr. Pye tried to get me in the Ottawa hospital. They had a new serum that might help, he said. The hospital was filled and it would be after the first of the year before they could admit me. In the meantime, Dr. Pye was in and out almost every day—constantly checking on my condition. No doctor could have shown more compassion.

Then late one Saturday night, the first week in January of 1963, I was sitting in the living room over the restaurant looking through the moisture-streaked window at the ice-covered lake across the highway. There was a heavy snow falling, and the lights from Clarence's station below cast an eerie glow in front of the restaurant. I could see him, wading through the snow, getting ready to close up for the night.

On the highway, a few slow-moving cars felt their way down the road, their headlights punching feeble holes in the swirling whiteness. I noticed one westbound car slowly creeping into the station, its windshield wipers vainly trying to clear the glass of the sticky, blowing snow. A dark figure got out and labored through the deep drifts toward the station door, overcoat buttoned high against his face and hat pulled over his eyes.

Moments later, I heard a stomping on the steps and a knock at the door. It was Dr. Pye. He pulled up a small stool and sat down in front of me. He had just driven in from Ottawa. There was still no word on when I could get in the hospital, but he had brought home some of the new serum. He had never administered any of it, but if I was willing to try, he could have me at the hospital in Pembroke the next morning and would give it to me himself.

Clarence had come up and was standing beside the door that led into the bedroom. I looked up at him. "What should I do?"

Dr. Pye looked at me and said, "Do not ask Clarence. This is something you must decide for yourself."

"Why?" I asked.

"Because from what we have found out about this new serum," he said seriously, "it could go one of two ways. Either it will make you better or you will get worse."

Worse? What if I did get worse? What if I had to go through another one of those horrible shaking spells?

"What would you do if you were in my shoes?" I asked Dr. Pye.

"I am not telling you what to do," he said, "but as far as I can see, you have nothing to lose."

At eight o'clock the next morning, Clarence bundled me up in my warmest clothes and carried me down the stairs to the car. It had stopped snowing and the early morning sun was peeking between the gray dawn clouds and reflecting off the glistening icicles that hung from the branches of the snow-ladened trees alongside the road.

Early on Monday morning they began the treatment. The process consisted of draining the fluid off my spine and replacing it with the special serum. It had to be administered without an anesthetic. "You will just have to tough it out, Mary," he said, "and let me know if I get too close to a nerve." It was extremely painful, but I tried to work with him day after day.

Each day he would test the reflexes in the lower half of my body to see if any of the sensation had returned. Nothing. "I am hoping when the feeling returns, you will be able to walk," he said. I could sense he was genuinely worried about the effects of the treatments. All this time, I kept asking myself, "Am I going to be able to walk or will I get worse?"

One night, about two months after the treatments began, I felt the prick of a hypo needle. I knew I was getting better. It was not long before I could feel the sheets on the bed. My sense of feeling was gradually returning. Although it never did return in my toes, I still felt like a whole person again.

If the sense of feeling has returned in my legs, then I ought to be able to walk, I thought. I began asking the doctor when he was going to let me try my legs.

259

It had been two and a half months since that early Sunday morning we had driven to Pembroke. Clarence had visited almost every day and Ona and the boys had been coming faithfully. I had been building up their hopes that I was soon going to be able to walk again. They, too, were waiting for the big day.

Finally, the time arrived when Dr. Pye told me I could test my legs. He helped me out of bed and I reached down and put my toes on the floor. "Now Mary, you will not feel your toes, but the rest of you is sound and whole and you should be able to make it," the doctor said.

Gradually I straightened up—and then collapsed forward into his arms. I could not hold myself up. The muscles refused to stiffen and respond. There was nothing. I tried once more before they helped me back into bed. It was a disappointing, depressing shock. That afternoon the nurse came through the door with what might as well have been my casket. It was a wheelchair.

I tried to keep it from my family. When visiting hours arrived. I had the nurses hide the wheelchair so they would not know I could not walk. But Ona seemed to sense something was wrong. Then she suddenly quit coming to see me.

One night, Barry came by himself and I asked him why Ona had not been over during the past week. In his innocent way he said, "It is all on account of you, Mom. Every since that night Dr. Pye came by the place and told Daddy you would never walk again, she has been like this. It is her nerves, I guess."

"Never walk again? You mean he said I would never walk again? And you have known all along that I have been in a wheelchair and have not said anything about it?" The shock of hearing the verdict was more than I could stand and I began to cry. Barry was embarrassed and hurt, but I was thankful it was all out just the same.

The next morning I asked Dr. Pye about it. He hung his head. "That's right, Mary. I did tell them. I did it to help Ona face reality. I am not saying you will never walk again. It is going to be a long time and the chances are mighty slim you will ever be back on your feet. But you can go home and we will get you a wheelchair."

Dr. Pye continued, "Now we are going to have to work together on Ona. You have been hiding your real condition from her. She cannot accept the fact you are an invalid because you will not face her with it. You have to smarten up, girl, and help her understand what lies ahead."

But I could not stand the thought of my daughter seeing me in a wheelchair. "I will try, doctor," I said, "but I just do not think I can do it."

Dr. Pye knew my problem and behind my back arranged to put me in a position where I would be forced to help Ona face reality. That night, one of the nurses came for me and wheeled me down to another patient's room to watch television. As visiting hours approached, however, I became more and more restless and finally buzzed for the nurse to come take me back to my room. "I have to get out of this wheelchair before my family arrives," I said.

She wheeled me out into the hall and then excused herself to run an errand. "Don't leave me here," I shouted after her. But she just walked off and left me.

Suddenly, I heard footsteps behind me. I recognized Clarence's heavy steps and the delicate clickety-click of Ona's heels on the hard floor. "What am I going to do?" I moaned. "Maybe they won't recognize me." I hung my head and hoped they would just walk on past.

Then I felt Ona's hand on my shoulder and heard her quivering voice. "Mum, what are you doing out here? Why did they leave you alone in the hall?" Before I knew it she was pushing me down the corridor to my room.

The nurse came in and said, "Now you just sit there in your wheelchair and talk to your daughter. You have not sat up in a long time." She left me with Ona sitting across the room staring at me in the wheelchair. It was a very silent visiting hour. We were all scared to talk for fear we would cry, so we just sat there looking at each other.

When she left, she bent over and kissed me. "It is not so bad, Mum. When you get home, I can wheel you around."

A week later, I was home—in the wheelchair. The boys came to my rescue and carried me up the stairs. And it was not long before I learned I could live an almost normal life from the wheelchair. I could do the mending. I could dry dishes. I could peel the potatoes and vegetables for the restaurant. I could clean the silverware and fold the napkins. I even got so I could run the vacuum cleaner. I was just as busy as everyone else.

At first, the boys carried me up and down from the restaurant, but I soon learned that I could sit on a piece of cardboard and slide down the steps. By holding onto the handrail I could drag my useless legs behind me and moving from one step to the other finally get to the top.

I was in the wheelchair until the middle of the summer. Then one day Clarence brought home a walker—a contraption designed to fit around me from three sides so I could lean on it and push it in front of me from a standing position. I found that by using my shoulder muscles I could pick up my legs. It was very awkward, walking with my shoulders. By hunching my left shoulder high in the air, I could bring my left foot up just high enough to make it swing forward. Then I would repeat the action with my right leg. By heaving my body into the air, I could make slow progress with the aid of the walker.

That fall I was finally able to stand alone. I could not make my legs go forward without the walker, but I could go backward. My boys would get on the floor and take turns holding the walker while the other one picked up my feet and moved them forward, trying to teach my feet to walk all over again using a different set of muscles.

Every night I would go to bed praying for God to help me. Then one morning I got up and automatically my foot went forward when I slipped out of bed. I screamed downstairs and my family came running up. "Look everyone, my foot went forward," I shouted. But when I tried to make it go forward again, it would not. What did I do to make it go forward the first time? Clarence and the three children were all standing around waiting anxiously. Finally, I was able to reconstruct the process in my mind and very slowly and deliberately I moved my foot again—forward. It was a happy day.

I still could not lift my toes. I could get my heels off the ground by jerking my shoulders into the air, but my toes would still drag as I walked. And, of course, I would stumble on the slightest bump or mound. By the end of the year, I was getting around pretty well on crutches or a cane—however, I was quite a sight to behold as I propelled myself forward.

During the next three years, I learned something else: the doctor was right with his first prognosis. I would get progressively worse. I would go for several months and make seeming progress, and then have another hard attack. Each attack was always a little more severe than the last and left me a little worse. Each time, it seemed, I would have to learn how to walk again when I got out of the hospital. I got so I dreaded seeing the sun come up on a new day for fear it would be the day of another attack.

The muscle spasms in my back were the worst. They began in the big muscles along the spinal column and moments later I would be completely out of control. I thought the shaking spasms were bad, but in comparison they were nothing. As the muscles contracted they drew my shoulder blades back until they almost touched. This threw my arms up and out and then my head was drawn backward toward my spine. I could not breathe. I had to gasp and cry out for each breath and sometimes I would even pass out from lack of oxygen. My legs were drawn backward and my heels pulled up toward the center of my spine until I was almost turned inside out.

It was after one of these horrible attacks that I was back in the hospital at Pembroke. I had lost all use of my backbone. The doctor said, "I am going to send you to St. Vincent's in Ottawa."

"Oh, no, you are not," I shot back at him from my prone position in bed. "That is for cripples who will never be anything but cripples and you are not going to put me there."

I could tell Dr. Pye was disgusted with me. "Mary, maybe they can get you to walking there. They have all the proper equipment."

"I will go home and stay until my family is tired of me and then I will go to St. Vincent's. But I am not going yet."

"But you cannot even go home now," he argued. "You cannot even stand up. Now just what do you think it would take to get you to walking again?"

I felt definitely that if he could find some means to support my spine, I could make my legs work. So I said in jest, "If you nailed a board to the back of my head and the other end to my bottomside I would be able to walk."

Dr. Pye gave me a strange look and turned and left the room. Thirty minutes later two nurses appeared with a stretcher. "Oh, no," I thought, "he is really going to nail a board to me." When I arrived in the surgical room, I found he was preparing a cast. It took them four tries and on the fourth they had to suspend me from a hoist and build the cast around me—but they finally got it done. And when they lowered me to the floor, I could stand and walk.

The months dragged by and they finally took the cast off and replaced it with shoes with iron leg braces. Sometimes I would have to wear a neck brace, too.

Dr. Pye thought we should close the restaurant. I knew he was right. It was far more than I could handle in the wheelchair. The hours were too long and the work too strenuous. So we closed the restaurant and I opened a small dress shop instead. I had to have something to do to occupy my time.

The spasms were coming more often and I was being carried to the hospital almost every third month to stay from two to three weeks. I had trouble with my throat and sometimes lost all sense of taste. Dr. Pye recommended physical therapy to try to improve my coordination. I was making regular visits to the physiotherapist in Cobden who helped with the exercise and treatments.

Murray was getting married in October, 1967. Of course, the entire family was involved in the wedding and they all insisted that I attend. I remembered that horrible incident at my uncle's funeral and told them I would just stay home and wish them Godspeed from there.

They finally persuaded me to attend. Barry was the best man. Ona was a bridesmaid. I made them promise they would not look at me after the service started. "Please, please promise me you will not look and if anything happens, just go on as if I were not even there." They all agreed.

When the wedding got underway and the group was all gathered at the front of the church, the shaking started. I was sitting with Clarence and next to my father on the second pew. The shaking was so bad I thought the pew would come unscrewed from the floor. The whole group of them turned around and looked at me and Helen, the bride, just shook her head. I was so embarrassed, I could have cried. After the wedding, I spent three more weeks in the hospital. I was getting pretty discouraged.

"I cannot go on like this," I thought afterward. "Something has to happen."

That something was just around the corner. It came in a visit from an older farm couple from Forester's Falls—the Kenneth Mays. The Mays lived across the road from my brother and his wife. Mrs. May had told them of her husband's miraculous healing of terminal cancer of the lymph glands. My brother had told her about me and asked if they would come see me. They did. They made several visits, sharing their experiences from the Kathryn Kuhlman services in Pittsburgh. "You will find out, just as I did, that God has the power to heal," he said.

I thought about it a lot, but could not make up my mind. It was all so strange—so different. We were all active in our little church, but I had just never considered such a thing as divine healing.

In June, 1968, we were invited to another wedding. "No!" I said steadfastly. "I have broken up my last public service." It was a favorite niece up in Kirland Lake, about 350 miles north of Pembroke. The family was all going and I finally agreed to go with them, but I was determined that I was going to sit in the car. Dr. Pye had given me some quick-acting pills that he said I could take if I felt the shakes coming on. The family encouraged me and I finally consented to go inside.

Once inside the church, we were separated. Murray and his wife were seated down near the front and she had the pills in her purse. Clarence and I were seated in the middle of a pew and Barry was several rows behind us. I had no sooner been seated than I felt my body begin to tremble.

"Clarence," I whispered, "I am getting the shakes. Get me out of here." It was too late. It was one of the worst spells I had had. Barry saw what was happening and got up and pushed his way over the people sitting around him and then trampled all over the people in our row as he wedged himself between me and the lady sitting beside me. Clarence was on the other side and the two of them tried to hold me still. It was horribly embarrassing, especially since I was in a strange place and the people did not understand my problem.

Murray and his wife turned round and she suddenly realized she had the pills in her purse. She gave them to Murray and he got up right in the middle of the wedding and walked back down the aisle to bring me the pills.

My heels were rattling against the wooden floor and causing an abominable noise. Clarence and Barry put their feet under mine and held me tightly. The pills began to take effect and made me drowsy, but the shaking continued. When the service was over, they picked me up by my elbows and carried me out. My legs were flopping in all directions and my head was jerking back and forth. Murray joined us at the door and they put me in the car and drove me to the hotel.

While I was sitting in church, I made up my mind that as soon as I got back to Cobden, I was going to make arrangements to go to Pittsburgh. Anything, just anything, was better than having to go through this again.

I called Mr. May as soon as I got back. He was thrilled over my decision and offered to take me. But Clarence said, "No, it is my job to see about your health. If that is what you want to do, then I will lock the garage and take you myself."

We were scheduled to leave on Wednesday at noon. "It seems a shame to drive all that way down by ourselves," I said to Clarence. "I have heard some of the other ladies say they wanted to go if anyone was going. Do you think we could make room?" So we wound up taking Mrs. Ross, Mrs. Smith, and her sixteen-year-old daughter, Pearlie, who had a spinal curvature.

We arrived on Thursday and, since we were all short of funds, decided to all crowd into one motel room. When we went to bed that night, we were all the model of modesty. First one of us would go in the bathroom and change into our bedclothes and then while the rest all turned their backs, we would dash for the bed and pull the covers up under our chins. But during the night, we forgot all about our modesty. We forgot it because I almost died of a back muscle spasm.

My body was convulsing so badly Clarence could not handle me. Everyone was flying around the room putting cold towels on my back and trying to straighten out my arms and legs and hold my head in position so I would not suffocate. It was not until it was all over that they remembered how careful they had been to keep from exposing themselves to each other earlier in the evening!

The next morning, July 12, was the day of the miracle service. As we left for Carnegie Hall I remembered it had been on July 12, six years before, that I had not been able to get out of bed for the first time. I found myself praying, asking God to do the miraculous and heal my body.

Mr. May had warned us to go in the side door. Clarence had intended to bring a folding chair so I could sit before the service began, but he forgot it and had to run down to a store and buy one after we got to the auditorium. When the doors opened, I was shaking so badly that I could not get up. An usher helped Clarence carry me inside and they placed my folding chair on the back row. Clarence took a seat directly in front of me.

Suddenly the service started. Miss Kuhlman appeared on the stage and all the people rose to their feet in song. I finally managed to stand, holding tightly onto the seat in front of me. Clarence turned and looked at me and begged me to sit down. But I could not. My body was so stiff it was impossible for me to sit back down. I felt like my hands were nailed to the seat in front of me.

"Please, Mary, sit down," Clarence whispered. But all I could do was stand as if glued to the spot—shaking. Suddenly, I felt a strange, electric-like tingling running through my body. It was a sensation not unlike others I had had before going into a spasm.

"Clarence," I whispered. He sensed the anxiety in my voice and left his seat and came back and stood beside me. "Get me out of here quickly; I am about to have another back spasm."

Having just gone through one the night before, Clarence knew what could happen and he motioned to a nearby worker. They led me out into the lobby which was filled with people. I reached the middle of the lobby when I passed out.

During the last three years, I had been having vivid dreams at night. I dreamed I was normal: walking, dancing, washing walls, making up beds, doing all the things I loved to do in life. I had so many of these dreams and they were so real to me that they made me depressed. When I awoke in the morning, I would lie in bed and cry because they seemed so real and I dreaded having to face another day.

Lying there on the floor of the lobby at Carnegie Hall, I had another such dream. As I regained consciousness, I felt myself trying to hold back. "No," I said to myself. "I do not want to go back to that world of pain and deformity. I want to remain here in dreamland where I am well and happy."

But consciousness slowly returned and I opened my eyes. There was a strange face in front of me. I did not recognize it. It was a crying face. I had only seen Clarence cry once in all my life. But it was Clarence and he was crying. Then it all came back to me. I closed my eyes and thought, I have to get up. When I opened them again, Clarence was smiling. He extended a hand to me and I came right up off the floor like I was a high school cheerleader.

I do not know who said it first, whether I said, "Clarence, I have been healed," or whether he said, "Mary, you have been healed." It makes no difference, for we were in each other's arms. This time we both cried.

Through my tears I said, "Clarence, I can feel my toes. I can feel them against the floor. I have ten toes and I can feel all of them." It had been five years since I had felt my toes against the floor.

I began to walk—normally. I could pick up my feet. I later realized I was talking loud, almost shouting. No telling how many people were disturbed in that meeting by all the commotion I was making back in the lobby.

They walked me out on the side porch and suggested I walk down the steps. They were concrete. I stood looking down those five steps toward the sidewalk which seemed to be hundreds of feet below. You cannot do that, I thought. You will fall and break your neck. But my feet kept right on going and I went down and up.

"Oh, Clarence, I wish the children were here. I wish they could see me now." I felt like shouting, "look everyone, I'm walking!" The three other women met me at the door. We stood there in the doorway laughing and crying and hugging each other. Then I was called to the stage and Miss Kuhlman insisted Clarence come up also. Suddenly both of us were under the power of God. "Oh, I wish the children could see me now," I kept saying.

We spent that night in Pittsburgh. For six years I had wanted to go shopping, but it had been impossible. This was my first trip to the States and I held Clarence to his promise that if I were healed, he would let me shop to my heart's content. That evening he took me to the biggest shopping center I had ever seen. "Buy anything you want," he said, smiling from ear to ear.

I walked and walked and walked some more. The shelves were piled high with wonderful things, but I did not see a thing I wanted. It seemed I had everything I could ever need. All I bought was a pair of sandals. For years I had had to wear those big, rough oxfords with the braces and now I wanted to be able to see my new toes.

We phoned the children from the motel room. They were all waiting for us when we pulled up the next evening in front of the station. "Hurry, get out. Let's see you," they shouted through the car window. They followed me up the stairs watching my feet and legs as they gracefully moved from one step to another. There was no trace of the disease left. We sat up most of the night trying to answer the hundreds of questions they were firing at us.

There were no answers to some of the questions. Dr. Pye just shook his head although he was very happy for me. My therapist said it was medically impossible.

But it happened. I cannot tell you how it happened or why it happened, but one thing I know—God did it!

Afterword

Those Who Are Not Healed

"Why are not all healed?" The only honest answer I can give is: I do not know. And I am afraid of those who claim they do know. For only God knows, and who can fathom the mind of God? Who can understand His reasoning?

I think there are some simple matters we can look into, but the ultimate answer as to who is healed and who is not healed lies with God alone.

Often there are those who come praying for physical healing and they get so caught up in the spiritual impact of the miracle service that they forget about their own need. They soon direct their prayers toward others and begin rejoicing over the miracles that take place. Oddly enough, it is often at this precise moment that God chooses to heal—when self is forgotten and God and others come first.

This was what happened in the case of Eugenia Sanderson, although she had also been praying and believing. But others, like Fred Burdick, are skeptics—hard-boiled unbelievers in miracles—yet they, too, are often healed.

Tiny Poor was healed without ever getting into the service, while there are many like Ritva Romanowsky, who are healed on the way to the service or like Kenneth May who are healed while waiting to get in. Freda Longstaff was healed in her home, and Nick Cadena left shaking his head, not realizing that the Holy Spirit had gone to work in his life and would eventually heal both body and soul. And who can figure out what happened to Mary Pettigrew? There is no understanding the mind and the ways of Almighty God.

There are thousands and thousands who can prove conclusively that Jesus has healed them and that His power remains the same and the faith that has in times past "subdued kingdoms, wrought righteousness, obtained promises, stopped the mouths of lions, quenched the violence of fire, escaped the edge of the sword...turned to flight the armies of the aliens"—that faith has done it again!

Yet, we must face facts. There must be a reason why some people are not healed; why there are those who insist that they have "all the faith in the world" and they leave the service in the same condition as when they came. The great tragedy is that discouragements ultimately come with disappointments.

We know from God's Word that a faith that weighs no more than a grain of mustard seed will do more than a ton of will or a mind of determination. The faith that Jesus talked about can no more manifest itself without result than the sun can shine without light and heat; but in many instances, people have mistaken their own ability to believe for the faith which only God can give! Faith is not a condition of the mind. It is a divinely imparted grace to the heart.

Our emotions and desires are often mistaken for faith and it is so easy to blame God when there are no results from something that has been purely of the mind and not of the heart. One of the most difficult things in the world is to realize that faith can be received only as it is imparted to the heart by God himself. It cannot be manufactured. No matter how much we nurture and cultivate that spirit that the world interprets as faith, it will never grow into the type of faith that was introduced by Jesus.

When we come to our salvation, it is still a matter of faith and, again, He gives us His faith to believe. "As many as received Him to them gave He power to become the sons of God, even to them which believe on His name."

The same Holy Spirit who convicts the sinner of his sins and sees to it that he is given enough conviction to convince him of his sin, will provide faith enough to convince him of his salvation. But no man in himself possesses that faith. It is given him by the same One who gives the faith for our physical healing: the Author and Finisher of our faith—Christ Jesus!

With Him there is no struggle! How often in a miracle service I have seen conscientious people struggling, straining, demanding that God give them the healing for their body, and yet there was no answer.

We can believe in healing. We can believe in our Lord and His power to heal. But only Jesus can work the work that will lift us to the mountain peaks of victory. We have made faith a product of a finite mind, when all of the other gifts of the Spirit we have attributed to God. To many people, faith still is their own ability to believe a truth, and is often based on their struggles and their ability to drive away doubt and unbelief through a process of continued affirmations.

There is belief in faith, but faith is more than belief. Faith is a gift. Jesus is our faith, and the Giver of every good and perfect gift is the Author and Finisher of our faith. Active faith is unquestioning belief, trust, and reliance upon God with all confidence. Faith can become as real as any of our senses. When we receive His faith, we also receive understanding. Everything that God has for His children, He puts within the reach of faith—then He turns around and gives them the faith to appropriate the gift.

Then Jesus spoke. With Him, there is no struggle and the waves of doubt and anxiety and worry all fade away and a glorious and marvelous calm and peace enter into the heart and mind of the one who has received that which only He can give. Then the only noise will be that of praise and adoration from the lips of the one who has just been healed by the Great Physician.

One of the greatest secrets that I have learned through the years is that when I have realized my own helplessness and have acknowledged it to Him, I have received some of the greatest manifestations of His power that I have ever experienced. You are nearest your possession of this imparted grace when you realize your own helplessness and your complete and entire dependence upon the Lord.

I am reminded of the young lady who, in describing faith, used this illustration. She said, "When I was learning to float on water, I realized I had to completely relax and without fear trust the water to hold me up—it worked. I floated—in the same way I faithed."

We receive nothing by demanding of God, but it is because of His great love, compassion, and mercy that

He gives to us. Often we lose sight of the fact that not one of us can claim any righteousness of our own, not one is worthy of the smallest blessing. We are the receivers of His blessing because of His mercy and compassion. *Healing is the sovereign act of God.*

When I was twenty years of age, I could have given you all the answers. My theology was straight and I was sure that if you followed certain rules, worked hard enough, obeyed all the commandments, and had yourself in a certain spiritual state, God would heal you.

Lo and behold, my theology came tumbling down and was crushed into a thousand pieces when one day a man who had just entered the auditorium during a miracle service stood silently against the back wall, and after not more than five minutes, walked boldly to the stage and freely admitted, "My ear has just opened and I do not believe!"

Although I questioned him repeatedly, he never recanted. Seeing the crowd, out of curiosity, he came in, not knowing whether it was an auction or some kind of giveaway program. He was standing there as a spectator and after much questioning, I found out that he had not been to church for more than twenty-five years and had put himself in the category of an atheist.

It is possible for me to relate many cases where people have been healed who were amazed, who freely admitted that they did not expect to be healed, who sobbingly cried, "I cannot believe it—I cannot believe it!" Until we have a way of defining it, all that I can tell you is that these are mercy healings. They have been healed through the mercy of the Lord.

We forget the mercy of God—we forget His great compassion—we forget that we do not earn our blessings; neither do we merit His goodness. Were it not for the mercy and the compassion and the grace and the love of God, not one of us would be a Christian and the same holds true when it comes to physical healing. How often I have thought that God cares very little about man's theology, and we are so prone to get dogmatic about things that we know so little about!

God never responds to man's demands to prove himself. I am amazed at the number of people who try to proposition God. But you cannot put God on the spot; you cannot say to Him, "I am not sure of You, but if You will heal me, *then* I will believe in You."

We have all heard of atheists who have attempted to disprove God by cursing Him and daring Him to strike them dead. Then when nothing happens, they loudly proclaim, "There is no God, else He would have struck back." But God cannot be manipulated.

Jesus recognized this when Satan tempted Him to throw Himself from the pinnacle of the Temple and proposition God to catch Him up. Satan even quoted Scripture to try to prove that God would answer such a presumptuous demand. But you cannot presume upon God. It is up to us to follow God, not demand of Him. God does not have to prove himself to anyone.

There are some things in life which will always be unanswerable because we see through a glass darkly. God knows the beginning to the end, while all we can do is catch a glimpse of the present, and a distorted glimpse at that.

If a man like Paul, after all his glorious revelations, did not have the answers for his own thorn in the flesh, then how can we expect to know the answers? God's answer to Paul is adequate to me, "My grace is sufficient for thee: for my strength is made perfect in weakness." Paul's answer to the world should become the password of every believer, "Most gladly, therefore, will I rather glory in my infirmities, that the power of Christ may rest upon me." In Nehemiah's time, when the people were sadly mourning, he said to them, "The joy of the Lord is your strength." That simply means, what pleases God is your strength.

In 1865, when Lincoln was assassinated—the great, patient, mighty Lincoln—an excited throng of thousands gathered in the streets of Washington. They were utterly bewildered, going to and fro as sheep without any shepherd. They were overcome by questions and emotions incident to that tragic hour. But in the midst of the tragic turmoil, a man appeared on the steps of the Capitol and said, "God reigns and the government at Washington still lives." The crowds dispersed quietly.

The right words had been said: *"God reigns!"*

A Message to the Reader of this Book:

Many of Kathryn Kuhlman's heart-to-heart radio talks are available on cassette and in book form. If you would like information on any of these, you may request a listing of the messages by writing to:

The Kathryn Kuhlman Foundation
P.O. Box 3
Pittsburgh, PA 15230